Lisa Roukin, a Le Cordon Bleu chef, and known also through 'Cook with Lisa', has been demonstrating healthy, contemporary cooking to London's young professionals, families and children since 2008. That same year she was a finalist on "The F Word" leading her to realise that she wanted to be her own boss in the kitchen!

Her career in the catering trade has included: Mirabelle, L'Escargot, Quo Vadis, The Ivy and Le Caprice. She currently provides the world's largest online supermarket, Ocado, with gluten free recipes.

Going forward, Lisa aims to continue on the healthy path she has found. Her emphasis also continues to be on creating nourishing recipes that encourage people of all ages and skill levels to cook together.

Second edition 2017

Author	Lisa Roukin
Photographer	David Munns
Prop Stylist	Victoria Allen
Food Stylist	Emily Kydd
Stylist	Jude Lobb
Make-up	Rina Steinberg
Hair	Carlos Alves
Food	Ocado
	Panzers Fruit
	Bifulco Butchers
	JA Corney Fish
	Menachems Butchers

Notes for the reader.

I have endeavoured to provide healthy gluten-free recipes. Gluten does appear in many guises and it will be up to you to check
labels. There are dishes containing dairy but I've designed them so you can omit them. As always, if you are concerned, check
with the manufacturer.

My aim is to reduce the amount of refined white sugars and there are only a handful of recipes that include icing sugar. Please
also note that some recipes contain nuts and should be avoided if you have an allergy.

Garnishes and serving suggestions are all optional and based on your preference, what works best for you. I have omitted using
white rice as brown is my preferred choice.

The times given in the preparation and cooking method are an approximate guide. Cooking times may also vary, you may need
to adjust the temperature according to your oven's manufacturers guide.

Printed and bound in Great Britain by CPI Group (UK) Ltd, Croydon, CR0 4YY.

Website reference
www.myrelationshipwithfood.com
www.cookwithlisa.com
www.foodphotography.co.uk
www.emilykydd.com
www.ocado.com
www.whatwearwhen.biz
www.makeupbyrina.com

ocado.com
The online supermarket

Thank you to ocado.com for kindly providing the fabulous ingredients to create all the recipes featured
in this cookbook. You can find a selection of my recipes at ocado.com/recipes (author 'Cook with Lisa'),
and you can order all of the ingredients at the touch of a button.

MY RELATIONSHIP *with* FOOD
100 recipes to nourish mind, body & soul

Dear Gill

I hope you enjoy the recipes!

Happy Cooking

Happy eating :)

Lisa
xOx.

Lisa Roukin

Dedication

My Relationship with Food is dedicated to my Mother and Father. With their patience and guidance, this dream of mine has become a reality.

To my Mother

Not only are you my best friend, I am extremely grateful for the incredible relationship we share. From a young child, I have watched you create wonderful, memorable family meals, which have brought smiles to all who ate them. I've always aspired to cook like you and bring happiness to all my nearest and dearest. I have fond memories of shopping for food and cooking with you and grandma. I am so grateful that three generations of us can still cook together. You've been a wonderful mentor to me both inside and out of the kitchen. I cannot thank you enough for your support, guidance, encouragement and love.

To my Dad

I am so proud that we have shared the journey of creating this book together. You have dedicated so much time ensuring that it highlights all the wonderful dishes you love. I have enjoyed you being with me every step of the way.

You gave me a wonderful childhood packed with sharing your LOVE of food at all meal times. Thank you for being my chief taster and the pillar of my support.

And most of all I am truly grateful to you both for letting me experiment in the kitchen.

Love, Lisa x

Contents

Introduction

This isn't an ordinary cookbook. Yes, there are delicious recipes, gorgeous photos and clear instructions. But that's where the similarity ends. This book is personal. It's my story of how I've been able to manage my relationship with food.

I can hear you saying 'relationship with food' what does that mean? But, think about it. Consider how often you've been sitting at a table and someone announces 'I don't eat meat', 'I've just lost three stone get that fudge cake away – quick!', 'I don't eat green vegetables' or admits that they weren't fed well as a child. These are all types of food relationships.

Now, think about a bad day at work and that desire to come home to a frozen triple-stuffed pizza and half-bottle of wine. Or remember being 'treated' with an ice-cream cone or a sticky pudding after an insipid school dinner? Food in these cases has altered from *sustenance* to *comfort*, and the relationship with food has shifted.

If a personal relationship goes wrong in your life, there are a number of steps - often painful ones - you can take to help you move on and regain your independence and self-esteem.

But if - like many of us - your relationship with food is not healthy, you have to face that 'relationship' at least three times a day for the rest of your life.

Worse yet, you have to decide what to put on your plate and in your mouth. You may have trouble when going out to eat with family or friends. But you don't have to continue like this.

Here's where I'd like to come in and change things.

I've gone through some tough food relationships, and as you read on, I'll share with you tips on becoming healthy and nourished. My journey isn't that unusual, but it does have a happy ending.

After all, it is not all about 'what' you are eating but how you can make small alterations to help your relationship with food become an enjoyable one.

Our journey starts here.

Lisa Roukin

My Relationship with food

Eat what nourishes your body, do what nourishes your soul, think what nourishes your mind.

If you have a healthy relationship with food, the above advice is wonderful. But what if you don't? There comes a time, especially in teenage years, when we realise that we can't control everything around us.

However, for some of us comes the understanding that we *can* absolutely control what we put into our mouths. We can change the way our body looks by eating less. We can control what the scales say. We can control how our jeans fit. Let's be honest, it is a powerful feeling.

But… It is lonely and restrictive.

It makes us angry because we are not enjoying what everyone else is eating. It takes so much energy and 'mind-time' to plan what we are going to eat and how we are going to avoid the spectre of unwanted calorie laden food. Imagine this unhealthy relationship with food continuing into adult years. There are calls to dinner party hosts asking what they are planning on serving at their party, there are demands for 'special' foods, there are avoidance tactics when birthday cakes appear or when alcohol is served. For me, for too long, this was my relationship with food.

Early years

In a light-hearted manner, my mother has said 'perhaps giving Lisa flour and butter to play with as a child wasn't a great idea'. She wasn't commenting on my baking skills, but the fact that early on I learned to love foods that would later negatively affect my life.

My early relationship with food was based on comfort and the need for internal nourishment. While I was raised in a very close family, I still had a void that needed filling. I was shy and with that I also lacked confidence. I found joy in helping (and snacking) in the kitchen where the atmosphere was warm and safe. Eating gave me comfort. So I did a lot of it. You can guess what came next. I became a fat child. In fact, when I was 13, I weighed as much as my father, 180 pounds!

Not unexpectedly, I was teased about my weight by my classmates. This made me unhappy and I ate even more. It wasn't a healthy cycle. In my teen years, I realised that I was hiding behind this weight and I set about doing something about it. My relationship with food changed. Food was no longer a comfort but became the enemy.

I turned my back on all the food items that had made me 'happy'. Worse yet, I couldn't see the difference between 'good' foods and those which had assisted in the weight gain. To me, food was my adversary and the only way I could 'win' was to be in control. For a short while, I was the victor. I changed from the overweight kid to the thin teenager. I got attention and I gained confidence.

I felt like the proverbial ugly duckling that turned into a swan.

But what I didn't realise was that this new relationship with food was actually controlling *me*. Being thin didn't seem enough – I needed to be thinner. I was so fearful of that 'fat child' reappearing that I stuck to my food avoidance and suffered.

Little did I realise that my new relationship with food was arguably more destructive than the overeating.

I wasn't clear about eating sensibly and I was excluding most food groups from my daily diet. At this stage in my life, I had a really negative outlook on food and, in turn, my actions deprived me of what I loved most in life – cooking, entertaining and relaxed eating with family and friends. I wasn't able to 'go with the flow' when attending family gatherings or going to restaurants, I always wanted to know: what the menu was; what I could eat; and how the food would be cooked. This need for control even extended to what time we would be eating! Often, I would get so frustrated with all the anxiety I was causing myself and everyone else with

my behaviour that I would end up not going out at all.

I was the one who lost out and it got to a stage where this unhealthy pattern was not benefitting my happiness at all. This bad food relationship meant that I was excluding myself from being with my family and friends and enjoying life.

Finally, I decided that enough was enough and something had to change.

I needed to understand why I was taking these negative actions, and like any relationship that is faltering, it was useful to think about 'why' my behaviour had evolved. I spoke to the people closest to me and was surprised at the level of worry I had caused. I considered my insecurities about being overweight, about not having the new friends I had made post-weight loss and the fear I had about becoming that 'ugly duckling' again if my new skinny status wasn't maintained. This wasn't an easy time and changes didn't happen overnight!

My career in food

My life took an unusual turn at this point. I understood I had issues regarding food and eating and yet cooking was at the core of my happiness! Ironically, my career had taken me into the catering industry and I had worked in some of London's finest restaurants including Mirabelle, L'Escargot and Quo Vadis. I even headed the events department at Le Caprice.

Yet, in private, I was struggling on a daily basis with this relationship with food – and I was always surrounded by it. The glamour of these jobs also meant that my appearance was even more important than before. I continued to obsessively struggle to find the balance between 'thin' versus 'happy'.

But then a little old lady changed my life. My grandmother. After a particularly stressful day, she asked me to sit down and tell me what was wrong. I told her about the confused feelings I had about eating, about work and my future. She looked at me and simply asked, 'What makes you happy?' I looked back at her and replied 'Cooking'. She smiled and simply said, 'Then cooking is what you should do!' With the support of my family, I enrolled at the prestigious Le Cordon Bleu cooking school and started on a road which would change my life.

For the first time, I realised that food preparation was only half the knowledge – I also needed to learn *how to eat*. In a professional kitchen, portion control is at the heart of preparation. You consider how food is presented. You learn about nutrients and about balancing not only flavours, but food groups. Slowly a new relationship with food was beginning to form, and it was an exciting and creative time.

I gradually realised that with my new food knowledge, I didn't have to choose between my ideal weight and being 'happy'. I could have both!

Through reading, experimenting and tasting, I had identified what worked best for me and my body; creating recipes that gave me the satisfaction and 'comfort' that I wanted, but were balanced and nutritious at the same time. Over the last few years, I am proud to say, my relationship with food has become what it should be.

Like I said before, these changes didn't happen overnight. It has taken time, but I'm there! You can be too.

A healthy relationship or let's say 'informal action plan'

Before we start, I would like to make the following statement: I am not a person who chomps on carrots asserting their superiority over cupcakes! This is not about a path to being thin it's about becoming healthy and nourished.

Although initially, it may sound like it is about 'excluding' foods, the core of the advice is about getting a balance and changing the way you approach eating.

Whether you've been diagnosed with coeliac disease, are gluten intolerant or want to transform your diet, my approach is simple, I want to share what has worked for me. In other words, you don't have to make all the decisions yourself. You don't have to read all the conflicting advice in health magazines. You don't have to make a vow never to eat chocolate cake again. I'm just suggesting that you tip your eating patterns towards 'healthy'.

What's healthy? Here's what I've found

Decrease

- refined sugar
- white starchy carbohydrates
- animal fat and cream
- 'rewarding' yourself with calorie-laden food
- giving yourself a hard time if you fall 'off the wagon'!

Increase

- cooking with colourful vegetables
- the amount you cook at any given time
- the variety and types of food you eat
- texture into your cooking by adding nuts and seeds
- time spent on yourself. Take a walk each day, sit in the sunshine, or just read a book in a quiet place

Taking Care of Yourself

You'll find in the 100 recipes contained here that I've focussed on dishes that do not contain gluten and an overload of carbohydrates or refined sugar. This style of eating has worked for me and I've found, with experimentation and sneaky 'market-research' on family and friends that you can still enjoy tasty, wholesome food without these ingredients.

There are technical and scientific reasons for these choices, but the main reason I've made this decision is that eating this way has made me feel better, lighter, more clear-headed. My energy levels have become steadier and I don't find myself with my head on the desk by 3pm! Furthermore, I haven't gained back the weight. A definite bonus.

I hope those of you who love gluten and all things starchy can find something to enjoy here too. I hope it encourages you to cut down on processed wheat and sugar. Do it. See how you feel. You won't feel worse… Trust me. You will only feel better.

Fortunately, there has been a rise in demand for healthier options and supermarkets, restaurants and even neighbourhood coffee shops are stocking larger selections of healthy products. This style of eating is not 'alternative' anymore but absolutely becoming mainstream.

"Take care of your body. It's the only place you have to live"

Your journey toward a healthy relationship with food: top ten tips

1. I CAN RESIST ANYTHING BUT TEMPTATION
Perhaps Oscar Wilde had a point, why keep unhealthy food in your house? Check all the labels of the food in your house. If 'sugar' is listed in the top five ingredients, throw it out! Instead, ensure you have your favourite ingredients available in your fridge and store cupboards. Check 'best by' dates, too.

2. PLAN AHEAD
The key to happiness in a gluten-free diet is planning. Without forward thinking, you will find yourself eating convenience foods in the shape of burgers, pizza, sandwiches or pre-prepared foodstuffs that will not only contain gluten but will undoubtedly be high in fat.

3. NOURISH YOUR MIND
De-clutter your thoughts with a silent break, walk or meditation.

4. GOOD FOOD IS Gluten-free
Vegetables and fruit do not contain gluten. Meat, poultry and fish don't contain gluten. We have an abundance of ingredients to cook with and even better, they're the kinds of foods we should be eating.

5. MAKE IT BIG
As convenience foods usually contain gluten, to avoid falling into the 'I'm hungry now and I don't have the patience to cook at 6pm' trap, I make a big batch of soup, about 10 portions. When it's ready I break it down into takeaway containers and freeze it. Puréed soups work best like pumpkin, parsnip or sweet potato. They are delicious and filling and can work well for lunches or dinners. Making your own food is definitely the way to go; aside from being cheaper, you have total control of what is going into your body.

6. BE AWARE
Conscious eating means eating foods that agree with your body. It is an inner wisdom of the body. It is your body communicating what is nourishing you and what is not. It is that simple.

7. ...IS ALL YOU NEED
Season everything with love, what you put in is what you get out.

8. THE ONLY WAY IS UP
One small positive thought in the morning can change your whole day. Eat clean, stay clean! Every new day is another chance to change your life.

9. ENJOY!
Start as you mean to go on, remember that eating should be an enjoyable process. Make it a regular habit to prepare your meals with time and relaxation. Be totally present with the preparation of your meals and don't do anything else at the same time. When you eat, only eat. Feel how the food tastes, smells, observe the colours, feel the different textures in your mouth.

10. FEEL
Perhaps the most intimate relationship each of us will ever have is not with another person - instead it's between our bodies and our food.

Meet Lisa Roukin
Your questions, my
personal experience.

Q. What inspired you to write this book?

After you've been on a hard journey, you want to share what you've learned. I see a lot of people struggling with their relationship with food and it's only natural to want to help. It was in this spirit that I found myself offering stories about my relationship with food to my cooking classes.

I'd also realised that this focus on healthy eating and exercise had worked for me for a number of years. I hadn't regained the weight I had lost. I still had the vitality I had when I began eating this way, and I had more than 100 recipes in my personal collection. A cookbook was a natural extension of all these things.

As a chef, I've gained experience in food preparation and menu planning. As a person, I've struggled with a bad relationship with food in the past. The cookbook details my journey towards healthy eating and my philosophy of nourishment which I've found strikes the best balance between food enjoyment and health.

We can all find happiness regardless of our weight or body shape – the key is finding a way of eating that benefits body, mind and soul. *Choose* to eat well.

Q. Earlier in this book, you talk about a 'bad relationship' with food. Bad relationships aren't that easy to break. How did you do it?

After I had lost the 4 stone as a teenager, I obsessed about my weight, constantly worrying about calories and becoming heavy again. In order to ensure that I had complete control over what I ate, I abstained from parties, social situations and even family meals.

Looking back, I lost out on a lot of good times. I finally sought help for my food issues and was advised to keep a notebook to write down my thoughts before and after meals. Slowly, I began to realize that I was using food as a reward. Experts agree that emotional eating is a habit, it is a behaviour we have learned, probably in childhood and it comes from the happy feelings connected to eating special or 'naughty' food.

But food is not naughty, it is not cheeky, it is not rebellious. Those things are emotions inside us. The food is just food. If this eating behaviour is learned, then it can be un-learned too. Problems with eating are rarely about the food itself. Emotional eating is not usually about greed, it is about fulfilling a different need.

Q. What do you think are some of the reasons for these unhealthy relationships with food?

The most common reasons for overeating are: to reward or 'treat' yourself; when you need love or attention; and to relieve boredom.

Emotional eating is not so much about what you eat; it is about when and why you eat. Ever scoffed a chocolate bar without even tasting it? Ever had a full meal, but then an hour later, you're nibbling and snacking on something else? You probably weren't hungry, but you were lonely, stressed, unhappy, or frustrated.

Comfort eating is not a new concept. Freud considered overeating to be the manifestation of a trauma or significant event in the oral stage of childhood development. Any woman who suffers PMT can relate to the concept of emotional (or hormonal) eating. And this is why diet plans often fail. I'm not knocking weight loss regimes or diet clubs. I think they all have a positive role to play and really do work for some people. I just don't think they are enough, because if you eat to negate your emotions, the counting calories will not work and the next time you go to a 'weigh in' you may add 'feeling guilty' or a 'bit of a failure' to those negative emotions because you didn't stick to the plan.

But overeating doesn't mean that you didn't know what to do, just that the eating was driven by an unconscious force, an inner voice you could not switch off. So, you go home, defiant and eat something bad. Not because you are hungry, but because you have an urge to fulfil that emotional need that hasn't been satisfied. This is a very negative cycle. For me, I learned early on that food was a reward.

I also know that an emotional low - like a relationship break-up, or being stressed at work, - can unconsciously lead to seeking something 'nice'. Something that tells me I am special, I am 'ok'. This is the merry-go-round I've fought to get off! Understanding the events leading to this bad relationship is key to taking back control of your eating habits. Writing it down helps you to see your patterns more clearly.

Q. Any advice for people who continue to struggle with these relationships with food?

Be patient and don't beat yourself up when you fall off the wagon. Make changes gradually and you are more likely to stick to them longer-term. For instance, you wouldn't wake up and run a marathon without months of training so why should you jump into a 'radical' diet and expect it to work immediately? Slowly start alternating better foods. 'Better' in this case means healthy - foods that won't give you energy spikes. Be good to yourself.

To start with, we all know that the best way to lose or maintain weight in a healthy, sustainable way is through a combination of diet and exercise. But for large numbers of us, that isn't as easy as it sounds. We know what we should be doing but we just can't find the willpower to make the change. And we don't need the large helping of guilt and failure that comes with not following a

diet! How many of us start the New Year with good intentions, but just a few weeks in, all it takes is a bad day at work, or cold, miserable weather and before you know it we are 'treating' ourselves to that takeaway for dinner because 'I'm too tired to cook'. I'll bet that sounds familiar, and that's because of both our relationship with food and lack of planning.

The best way to succeed is to be organised. Ensure that the food that is good for you is actually in the house! Try slowly decreasing the amount of refined sugar and flour you have in your diet. Experiment with the time of day you eat and the quantity you eat. Listen to your body.

Q. Almost all the recipes in the cookbook are gluten-free. What is the thinking behind this?

While I am not a dietician, I've experienced the many health benefits of eating a cleaner and gluten-free diet. I'm now embracing the elimination of wheat/gluten. I want to educate people to understand that you can still make wonderful, tasty and wholesome looking dishes using wheat-free substitutes for favourite foods and sleep well knowing that they are full of goodness! Not every dish you make has to get its carbohydrates from starches since fruits and vegetables contain forms of them.

I hope that those of you who love gluten and all things starchy can find something to enjoy here, too. It may even encourage those with weight/digestion problems, poor skin, and little energy or low immune systems to cut out/cut down on gluten. Trust me you will only feel better.

Q. Here's the tough question, if you are not eating bread, what do you have for breakfast?

No excuses! Try Coconut Porridge, Israeli Salad with scrambled eggs, or Bircher Muesli. You could also be a bit radical and have a vegetable omelette or a frittata with quinoa. In some Mediterranean countries they eat eggs, olives and tomatoes for breakfast and in the Far East, they even have chicken soup! Small changes can improve your energy levels a lot. Breakfast is the perfect time to set a good standard for the day ahead.

Q. Now for an even harder question, how do you ensure you eat healthy food when you are going out for dinner or to someone's house? What if you are handed a piece of cake at someone's birthday party?

If you go out, stick to protein and vegetables. For example, have grilled chicken with salad at lunch or ask for cooked vegetables at dinner. You can even do this with a hamburger – just skip the bun and ask for salad instead of chips. Most restaurants will deal with this request without extra charges or hassles (it doesn't cost them any extra which is half the battle!).

You can even go out for a Sunday lunch – just skip the potatoes & Yorkshire pudding and you can eat everything else (you may want to ask if the gravy is gluten-free if you have allergies).

Just be sure you haven't waited too long to eat. If you have, it will be much harder to refuse the basket of bread. Once again, plan ahead.

Look for menu items which feature texture – such as salads with nuts. At home, fill your plate with colourful vegetables. Soon you will see eating sweet potatoes and red peppers as 'treats' because if you reduce your sugar intake – you'll notice how naturally sweet nature can be! As far as that birthday cake is concerned, the trick is to be gracious. "It looks delicious, but I've decided to go wheat free.'

Or, if it is a good friend, try the truth. "I find it difficult keeping a healthy balance in my life, please don't tempt me."

Q. When you entertain at home, do you stick to a gluten-free menu?

Yes. When the food is fresh, healthy, nutritious and delicious, people don't notice! In fact, the usual reaction is 'I've never had this before, may I have the recipe?'

The Non-Cheater's 'Cheat Sheet'

Another secret to having a good relationship with food is knowing how to substitute 'healthy' foods to satisfy cravings. The hard part is knowing what to substitute.

To make it easier for you to use this book, here are some healthy alternatives to some of the most commonly requested dishes. Soon I hope, you'll be craving the new dishes instead! Remember - plan ahead and have as many of the recipes that store well on-hand in case hunger strikes without warning! I always have homemade bircher muesli in the fridge for when I just *need* something sweet and quick!

I really want	I'll try this instead
French Toast with Maple Syrup	Bircher Muesli, Homemade Granola or Individual Granola & Berry Pots
English Fry Up	Shakshuka or Baked Eggs in Portabello Mushrooms
Macaroni Cheese	Courgette Spiralised Spaghetti with Aubergine Sauce
Deep Fried Chicken	Baked Cornflake Chicken Breast with Pan Fried Jersey Royals with Shallots & Rosemary
Pizza with Pepperoni	Cauliflower Pizza Base with Blue Cheese Walnut & Pear
Four Cheese and Mushroom Tart	Courgette & Shiitake Mushroom Quinoa Frittata
Deep Fried Courgette/Zucchini	Oven Baked Asparagus in Parmesan & Almond Crust
Bag of Crisps	Baked Curly Kale or Brussels Sprout Chips
Bar of Milk Chocolate	Raw Chocolate Brownie
Sticky Toffee Pudding with Custard	Lemon and Almond cake
Ice Cream Sundae	Banana Ice Cream with Halva
Cheesecake	Raw Blueberry Cheesecake

SPRING

seasonal moods

Revive! Like a door opening onto a brightly lit stage, spring arrives. There's real drama as the first brightly coloured flowers surface and the lightest of green leaves appear on trees. The sky becomes clearer and brilliant blue again.

And with the additional sunshine comes a new harvest: the annual wonder of fresh asparagus as their tiny verdant heads reach through the soil to the warmth above; cauliflower, like a vegetable bouquet, is also in season with its versatile personality. It's 'A' list friend, kale, packed with flavour and goodness adorns grocers' shelves.

Menus become lighter with the lifting of mood and it is also a time devoted to regaining energy. Spring is a time to 'clear out', de-clutter and get rid of anything that you no longer need or want. Embrace and allow the energy of new beginnings to flow in.

BANANAS They are the most popular fruit in the UK and a powerhouse of nutrition – high in potassium, B6 and magnesium. Try freezing them for the ultimate smoothie ingredient.

MINT There are 25 different species of mint but all have the cool, fresh scent which is instantly recognisable. As a food, the benefits of mint are often linked to the stomach, not least because it can relieve the symptoms of indigestion and muscle spasms.

CASHEWS Not only delicious as a snack or garnish, cashews also have a lower fat content than most other nuts, with over half their fatty acid content appearing as heart-healthy monounsaturated fats, similar to those found in olive oil. Makes wonderful nut butter, too!

ALMONDS Originating in the Middle East in both sweet and bitter varieties, almonds are particularly good for you. They are high in calcium - great news for anyone who doesn't eat dairy products.

QUINOA Pronounced keen-wah, technically quinoa is not a true grain but a seed related to spinach and Swiss chard. In food preparation think of using it in the same way you would rice. It is a powerhouse of nutrition containing protein, calcium, iron, vitamin E and B vitamins.

KALE If there could ever be such a thing as an A-list vegetable then it has to be kale. It's loved by nutritionists for its high calcium, vitamin K, vitamin C and omega-3 fatty acid content. No wonder it has been touted as the best green veggie around.

CAULIFLOWER Mark Twain called it 'broccoli with a college education' but cauliflower also offers 80% of your daily requirement of vitamin A. Try it in curries, salads and shaved finely with a touch of flavoured oil.

ASPARAGUS British asparagus is worth waiting for as its flavour is hard to beat. When shopping, look for tightly furled tips and shoots that are straight and firm.

Banana & Chia Seed Pancakes

Perhaps my ultimate challenge - creating
pancakes without flour & sugar!

....

{makes 6 pancakes}

for the pancakes

2 large bananas, (mash 1½ of
the bananas, keep ½ banana for
garnish)

2 large eggs, beaten

1 tsp chia seeds

2-4 tsp coconut oil (virgin or
odourless)

2 pinches salt

½ tsp baking powder, gluten-free

garnish

½ banana, sliced

blueberries

agave nectar, honey or maple syrup

2 handfuls pecans, crushed

Preparation time - 20 mins, cooking time - 20 mins

Mash ¾ of the bananas until smooth, then add the egg and beat
well.

Stir in the chia seeds, baking powder and salt and leave to rest for
5 minutes.

Heat a non-stick frying pan on a high heat and place a touch of
coconut oil to both the pan and a spatula (coating the spatula will
help when turning over the pancakes).

Turn the heat down to medium, pour a circle of the batter into the
pan. I use about 60ml of the mixture per pancake.

Cook until golden brown on the underside (approx. 1 minute), then
flip over and cook until golden brown on the other side (about 30
seconds).

Once you've cooked all 6 pancakes, stack them back on top of each
other to warm through in the hot pan, but take the pan off the heat.

Serve warm with the sliced banana, blueberries, crushed pecans and
agave nectar.

Yum...

LISA'S TIP

*My favourite food of all time? Pancakes. Hands down. But traditional
pancakes aren't exactly nutritious. So I wanted to figure out an
alternative! Eggs and a banana…. that's all! Two of my favourite
foods come together to create a simple, yet scrumptious pancake. It's
hard to believe that you don't need flour, milk or refined sugar to
create a lovely, light and kid-approved pancake. Although delightful,
don't be expecting your run-of-the-mill carb-filled pancake. These
have more of an eggy crepe-like texture, which is equally appealing.
If you're used to eating clean healthy foods, you will more than likely
LOVE these. Low-calorie, high-protein, grain free, gluten-free and
wheat-free…. what's not to love? Not only do they make a quick and
easy breakfast, but they're also the perfect pre- or post-workout fuel.
Try adding some other types of berries and nuts. Be adventurous
with your fillings or just keep it plain and simple! You could also
double up the baking powder if you would like them slightly thicker.*

Almond Milk

Nut milk is heavenly – sweet, mild
and gentle on the belly.

....

{makes a little over a litre}

ingredients

200g almonds with skins or
without (water for covering
almonds when soaking)

1 litre cold water

3-4 Medjool dates, pitted (optional)

2 tsp sweetener like agave nectar
honey, or maple syrup (optional)

1 tsp vanilla bean paste or vanilla
bean pod, deseeded (optional)

Preparation time - 30 mins, soaking time - 2 days or overnight

Soak the almonds overnight or up to 2 days with enough water to
cover. The longer the almonds soak, the creamier the almond milk
will be. Once the almonds have finished soaking, discard the liquid
then rinse the almonds thoroughly under cool running water.

Combine the almonds and a litre of water in a blender.

Blend at the highest speed for 2 minutes then pulse the blender a
few times to break up the almonds (add the dates if using), then
blend continuously for two minutes.

The almonds should be broken down into a very fine meal and
the water should be white and opaque (if using a food processor,
process for a total of 4 minutes, pausing to scrape down the sides
halfway through).

Line a strainer with either the opened nut bag or cheese cloth and
place over a tall measuring jug, then pour the almond mixture into
the strainer.

Press all the almond milk from the almond meal, gather the nut bag
or cheese cloth around the almond meal and twist tight.

Squeeze and press with clean hands to extract as much almond milk
as possible (Oh, and don't forget to keep your almond pulp. There's
no use in wasting any of that goodness…).

Taste the almond milk, and if a sweeter drink is desired, add your
desired honey or syrup to taste, together with the vanilla bean paste
if required.

Store the almond milk in sealed mason jars in the fridge for up to
two days.

LISA'S TIP

*This almond milk is light enough to serve as a neutral base in
smoothies and best of all, it digests seamlessly — unlike conventional
dairy, which so many among us (especially those of you who are
lactose intolerant) find difficult to stomach. Homemade almond milk
only lasts a few days in the fridge; so make just what you think you
will drink in this time period. Before serving, give the milk a gentle
stir as it can separate. The almond pulp that you put aside can either
be used in biscuits or homemade bread, or use it as an exfoliating
face scrub! Just add half the amount of oil to the mixture, coconut oil
is my preferred choice!*

Cashew Butter

Homemade nut butters not only taste better but enable
you to control levels of fat, salt and sugar.

{makes 500g of butter}

ingredients

500g cashew nuts, roasted or raw
(see Lisa's tip for roasting)

2 tsp agave nectar, honey or
maple syrup

2-3 pinches of sea salt

to serve

serve with gluten-free wholegrain
bread

Preparation time - 15-20 mins, cooking time - 13 mins (if you want to roast the cashews)

Add all the cashew nuts to the bowl of your food processor and process for 10-15 minutes, or until nice and smooth. It's a good idea to give your food processor a few minutes break from time to time.

At some point, you will have to scrape the sides fairly often, and your nuts will turn into a very thick and crumbly paste.

Although it will take some time and you might think that there's no way your nuts are EVER going to turn into butter – they eventually start to release their oils and turn into nut butter.

Be patient and resist the urge to add any form of liquid, a ball will form, but just let the food processor continue doing its job and you will get nice smooth butter!

Just before the end when you reach the consistency you like, add the sea salt and maple syrup or agave nectar.

Keep your nut butter in an air tight container for up to several weeks, if it hasn't been eaten long before then!

LISA'S TIP

You can roast the cashew nuts for approximately 13 minutes, prior to processing, to give that extra nutty flavour. Careful not to burn them! If you want to add a little twist, separate half of the mixture and add 3 tsp cocoa powder to one half... and give it a quick blend. Now, you can go and grab a spoon for a nutty chocolate fix!

Coconut Porridge

The addition of coconut makes this breakfast staple a
little less ordinary – and better for you, too!

....

{serves 2}

ingredients

570ml coconut water

80g porridge oats fine or rolled
(gluten-free)

garnish

1 large handful toasted coconut
chips

1 banana, sliced

cinnamon

agave nectar, honey or maple syrup

Preparation time - 10 mins, cooking time - 5 mins

Place the coconut water and oats in a non-stick saucepan and bring
to a boil, stirring often. Simmer for 3 minutes, occasionally stirring.
Leave to sit for 1 minute off the heat.

Toast your coconut chips, in a dry frying pan.

Serve with toasted coconut chips, sliced banana, cinnamon and
touch of agave syrup, if required.

LISA'S TIP

*This is a must-try porridge. It's healthy, nutritious, delicious and a
good source of potassium not just from the banana but also from
the coconut water, bursting with natural occurring electrolytes. I like
to serve the porridge inside a coconut shell and vary the toppings
to include blueberries, strawberries, chia seeds, or a nice dollop of
cashew butter!*

Heirloom Tomato, Puy Lentil & Halloumi Salad

This is a super simple dish that has a great balance between textures
and flavours – salty halloumi, earthy lentils and sweet, juicy tomatoes.

{serves 4}

ingredients

2 heirloom tomatoes, each cut into
4-5 slices

150g cherry tomatoes, cut in half

1 large courgette, julienned with
vegetable peeler (or vegetable spiral
cutter)

¼ red onion, sliced half moons

1 avocado, cubed

100g puy lentils (pre-cooked)

250g halloumi cheese, cut into 10
slices

1 large bunch chopped coriander

2 ½ tbsp olive oil

½ tbsp balsamic vinegar

½ tbsp agave nectar, honey or
maple syrup

sea salt and black pepper

garnish

fresh coriander or parsley

Preparation time - 40 mins, cooking time - 10 mins

Peel the courgette using a julienne vegetable peeler or spiraliser.

Using a non-stick frying pan, add the halloumi in two batches. Cook
on a medium heat on each side for about 2 minutes until lightly
browned. Place on a plate to cool and drizzle 1/2 tbsp agave nectar,
honey or maple syrup.

In a large mixing bowl add the cherry tomatoes, puy lentils, onion,
coriander, avocado, courgette spirals and season with sea salt and
black pepper.

Toss the salad lightly with 2 tbsp olive oil and ½ tbsp balsamic
vinegar.

On a serving platter, lay out the heirloom tomatoes placing the
mixed salad over the top.

Scatter the halloumi around the salad and garnish with coriander.

LISA'S TIP

*I always keep halloumi in the fridge since it has a long shelf-life.
Works well with added cucumber, pesto, olives... basil instead of
coriander, feta instead of halloumi, whatever you fancy. The halloumi
and tomatoes are robust enough to work brilliantly with a wide
variety of vegetables and herbs. Try spiralising carrots, beetroots,
parsnip and maybe a daikon radish. Get creative!*

Quinoa with Shiitake & Oyster Mushrooms

A tasty side dish or perfect as a main meal on a spring day.

{serves 4-6}

ingredients

225g quinoa, rinsed

450ml cold water

200g fine trimmed green beans, finely chopped

150g shiitake mushrooms, sliced

150g oyster mushrooms, sliced

2 tbsp groundnut oil or sunflower oil

1 tbsp sesame oil

4 tbsp tamari soy sauce (gluten-free)

4 tbsp agave nectar, honey or maple syrup

2 pinches sea salt

garnish

fresh coriander

sesame seeds, toasted

Preparation time - 40 mins, cooking time - 20 to 30 mins

Rinse the quinoa, through a fine sieve for about 1 minute.

In a medium saucepan add the quinoa and cold water, bring to a boil then place the lid and simmer on a low light for 20 mins.

When cooked, remove from the heat and leave to stand for 10 minutes, then lay the quinoa on a large plate to cool down.

Blanch the green beans in boiling salted water for 5 minutes then immerse into cold water to stop the cooking process. Chop finely.

In a large non-stick frying pan, add the groundnut or sunflower oil and sesame oil, then the sliced shiitake and oyster mushrooms, sauté until wilted for about 5 minutes, then add the tamari soy sauce and agave nectar, honey or maple syrup and simmer for 5 minutes.

Add the cooled quinoa to a large mixing bowl with the finely chopped green beans and mushrooms and mix together.

Check for seasoning then garnish with the sesame seeds and coriander.

LISA'S TIP

This quinoa salad with mushrooms and Asian flavours has quickly become one of my new favourite recipes. My relationship with quinoa got off to a rocky start last year but once I gave it another chance and cooked it correctly, I was hooked. High in protein and gluten-free, quinoa is way healthier than white rice/pasta so you don't even need to feel bad about grabbing seconds (or even thirds). Serve with poached eggs for extra protein.

Asian Salmon Fish Cakes

These are time-consuming to make, but the result never fails to please. If you are planning a party, make the fishcakes smaller and top with sweet chilli sauce for an impressive starter.

....

{serves 4 - makes 8 fishcakes}

ingredients

500g fresh salmon fillets, skinned

500g King Edward potatoes, peeled and cut into quarters

¼ tsp white peppercorns

1 tbsp white wine (optional)

2 shallots (60g), finely chopped

1 tbsp coconut oil (virgin or odourless)

1 egg yolk

1 ½ tbsp tomato ketchup

1 tsp Dijon or English mustard

2 tsp anchovy essence

1 tbsp sweet chilli sauce

5g coriander, chopped

cornflour for dusting

sea salt

white pepper

for coating and frying

250g medium cornmeal

2 eggs

cornflour for dusting

250-300ml groundnut (or rapeseed) oil

sea salt

white pepper

1 tsp garlic granules

garnish

2 tbsp mayonnaise

1 tbsp sweet chilli sauce

1 tsp ketchup

lemon wedges

rocket

Preparation time - 60 mins, cooking time - 40 mins

Poach the salmon by placing it in a medium-size pan with enough water to cover. Add the white peppercorns and white wine, bring to the boil, then turn off the heat. Cover and leave to stand for 10-15 minutes (depending on the size of the salmon fillets) to cook through. Now remove skin and any grey flesh. Separate the salmon into two equal sections and leave to cool.

Place the peeled and cut potatoes into a medium saucepan, cover with water and bring to the boil. Cook for 15-20 minutes then drain and mash the potatoes (for best results use a ricer).

Sauté the shallots in the coconut oil, season well with sea salt and white pepper. In a large mixing bowl, add the mashed potato, sautéed shallots, egg yolk, anchovy essence, ketchup, Dijon mustard and sweet chilli sauce and mix. Check for seasoning and add more of the sauces if needed.

Carefully flake one section of the salmon (the salmon will naturally flake) finely and shred the other half. Now add the finely shredded salmon to the potato mixture, then gently fold in the flakes along with the chopped coriander. Lightly dust a large chopping board with cornflour and season with sea salt and white pepper. Shape the mixture into 8 moulds, lightly dust with the cornflour on both sides then chill in the fridge for 30 minutes. Mix the mayonnaise with the sweet chilli sauce and ketchup for the garnish.

Mix the mayonnaise with the sweet chilli sauce and ketchup for the garnish.

Season the beaten eggs with sea salt, white pepper and garlic granules. Dip the fishcakes first into the egg then coat in the medium cornmeal. Heat 1cm of groundnut or rapeseed oil in a large frying pan (make sure that the oil doesn't get too hot). Fry the fishcakes in two batches for 3-4 minutes on each side or until they are golden, crisp and heated through. Drain on a kitchen towel. Serve with rocket, lemon wedges and the mayonnaise dip.

LISA'S TIP

You can make these fishcakes in advance and then preheat the oven to 375°F, gas mark 5, 190°C (170°C fan assisted) and heat for 10 minutes, then serve!

Massaged Curly Kale Salad

An unusual dish that has the new 'A' list vegetable, kale and
the benefit of creamy avocado and cool green grapes.

{serves 6 - 8}

ingredients

200g sliced curly kale (washed),
hard stalks discarded

300g fine trimmed beans,
finely chopped

1 avocado, cubed

½ lemon, juice only

2 tbsp extra virgin olive oil

150g green grapes, cut in half
lengthways

50g pistachios, roughly chopped

1 handful sesame seeds, toasted

sea salt

dressing - mint sauce (you will only need half)

10g mint, fresh

10g coriander, fresh

1 garlic clove

100g fat free Greek or soy yogurt
(or coconut milk)

1 tsp agave nectar, honey or maple
syrup

1 ripe mango

sea salt and black pepper

garnish

50g pistachios, roughly chopped

1 handful toasted sesame seeds

Preparation time - 30 mins, cooking time - 5 mins

Bring a medium pan of salted water to the boil, cook the fine trimmed green beans for 5 minutes, then drain and run under running cold water, then chop into small pieces, set aside.

To make the dressing, in a blender add the mango, mint, coriander, garlic clove and pulse then add the yogurt or coconut milk.

Season with sea salt, black pepper and 1 tsp agave nectar, honey or maple syrup.

In a large mixing bowl place the kale, add the lemon juice, olive oil and then add sea salt. The salt flavours the kale and also helps soften it by drawing out the water.

Using clean hands, massage the kale, working it until the colour deepens and it feels soft and tender. This process should take around 2 to 3 minutes.

At this point, stir in the remaining ingredients, avocado, grapes and beans.

Mix well, cover and let sit for an hour before serving to let the flavours infuse together.

Serve on a large flat platter.

Sprinkle the top with roughly chopped pistachios and toasted sesame seeds.

Drizzle half of the mint dressing over the salad. Keep the remaining dressing in the fridge.

LISA'S TIP

Raw, massaged kale salad is one of my very favourite foods in the entire world - one that would definitely be on my last meal list, and a special friend of mine Daniel would agree too! The bottom line is, once you learn the massaging technique, which softens the crunchy kale, you'll find yourself improvising versions of this salad left and right. When kale is massaged, its cellulose structure breaks down and wilts, so the leaves that were once tough and fibrous become silky. The kale reduces in volume by over half and the leaves take on a subtle sweetness.

Spring

Lamb Chops with Coriander & Mint

Mint is a classic accompaniment to lamb for a reason. Its fresh, cleansing taste is a natural foil to the heavier flavour of the charred meat.

{Serves 2-3}

ingredients

6 lamb cutlets, individual, French trimmed

marinade

1 handful fresh mint

1 handful fresh coriander

2 garlic cloves

4 tbsp olive oil (a little extra for frying)

2 tbsp sushi seasoning vinegar

2 tbsp sweet chili sauce

2 tbsp water

1 tbsp tamari soy sauce (gluten-free)

1 tbsp honey, agave nectar, or maple syrup

sea salt and cracked black pepper

Preparation time - 20 mins, cooking time - 8 to 10 mins in frying pan or 15 mins in oven. Marinating time - 4 hrs or overnight

Blitz all the marinade ingredients in a food processor. Taste and adjust sweet/sour/saltiness to perfection.

Place the lamb chops in a food bag and pour in the marinade, tie the bag up and leave to marinate for 4 hours or overnight is best.

Take the chops and marinade out of the bag, pour the sauce in a small saucepan, and gently heat.

Fry the lamb on a medium heat with a little oil, about 7-9 minutes (4 minutes on each side) and more if you prefer it well done; go to a maximum of 10 minutes.

Serve with the sauce drizzled over the cooked lamb chops.

LISA'S TIP

If you prefer you can heat the oven to 400°F/ 200°C (180°C fan assisted) Gas Mark 6. Heat up a heavy cast iron griddle, then lift the meat out of the marinade, shaking off the excess liquid. Reserve the sauce from the marinade to heat separately. Sear well on all sides, then transfer to a baking tray and cook in the oven for about 15 minutes, depending how big your cutlets are and how you like your meat cooked. Reduce to 10-12 minutes if you like them pink. I would serve these delicious chops with mange tout, peas and broccoli.

Quinoa Sushi Salad

All the flavours of traditional sushi but in a
salad with beautifully contrasting colours.

....

{Serves 4-6}

ingredients

250g quinoa, rinsed

450ml cold water

2 sweet potatoes

2 tbsp extra virgin olive oil

4 tbsp sushi seasoning vinegar

3 large eggs, beaten

1 tbsp coconut oil (virgin or
odourless)

2 tsp palm or coconut sugar

½ cucumber, deseeded and cut into
very small pieces

1 avocado, cut into small cubes

2 nori seaweed sheets, cut into
small strips (best to use kitchen
scissors)

1 handful chives, finely chopped

1 tbsp sesame seeds, toasted

2 tbsp sunflower seeds, toasted

1 tbsp tamari soy sauce or teriyaki
(gluten-free)

sea salt, cracked black pepper and
white pepper

garnish

tamari soy sauce or teriyaki
(gluten-free)

Preparation time - 60 mins, cooking time - 30 to 40 mins

Preheat the oven to 350°F, gas mark 4, 180°C (160°C fan-assisted).

Peel and cut the sweet potato into finger size strips, then place on
a baking tray lined with parchment paper or use a silicone baking
mat, drizzle with olive oil and season with sea salt and black pepper.

Bake in the preheated oven for 30 minutes, then remove from the
oven to cool.

Place the quinoa in a sieve and rinse under cold running water for
1 minute, then place in a saucepan with 450ml of cold water and
bring to the boil. Cover and simmer on a low heat for 20 minutes.

After 20 minutes, remove from the heat, carefully fluff with a fork,
then leave to settle for 10 minutes with the lid on.

Pour the quinoa onto a large platter and coat with sushi seasoning
vinegar.

In a dry non-stick frying pan toast the sesame and sunflowers seeds,
until lightly golden.

To make the omelette, beat the eggs and season with sea salt, white
pepper and palm sugar.

Melt the coconut oil in a non-stick frying pan and make the
omelette. Place on a plate to cool once cooked.

When the sweet potato and omelette has cooled, cut into small
cubes.

Add the cooled quinoa to a mixing bowl, add the sweet potato, egg,
cucumber, seaweed, toasted sesame seeds, sunflower seeds and
chives and stir gently until mixed.

Carefully fold in the avocado.

Drizzle over with either gluten-free teriyaki or tamari soy sauce

LISA'S TIP

*This lovely salad was created one day when I had full intentions of
making quinoa sushi. Just as I was about to get rolling I realised I
had run out of nori seaweed sheets. Then, I had a flash of brilliance,
SUSHI SALAD! I thought, throw everything together in a bowl,
AMAZING! The resulting salad was tangy, filling, complex, delicious,
and healthy too.*

Chicken Satay Skewers with Spicy Peanut Sauce

This Indonesian dish is a good introduction to Asian cooking
and the use of peanut butter is always surprisingly delicious!

{Serves 4-6}

ingredients

500g chicken breast, thinly sliced
into 2.5cm x 5cm slices
8-10 wooden skewers, soaked in
water

marinade

1 tsp ground cinnamon
1 tbsp ground cumin
1 tsp ground black pepper
150ml peanut oil
100ml light soya sauce
2 tbsp palm sugar or agave syrup

spicy peanut sauce

4 tbsp crunchy peanut butter
6 tbsp coconut milk
1 small lime
1 garlic clove, crushed
½ tsp curry powder, mild Madras
2 tsp sweet chilli sauce
1 tsp agave syrup
sea salt and ground white pepper

garnish

½ cucumber shredded
1 red onion, roughly chopped
baby cos lettuce
handful crushed peanuts
fresh coriander, for serving
lime wedges, for serving

Preparation time - 40 mins, cooking time - 10 to 12 mins (plus 4 hours or overnight marinating)

Put the chicken slices into a bowl and add all marinade ingredients. Stir thoroughly to make sure that all the chicken pieces are coated.

Leave for a minimum of 4 hours in the fridge, preferably overnight, giving it an occasional stir.

Place the coconut milk, peanut butter, and crushed garlic in a saucepan over a gentle heat for about 2 minutes, using a whisk to combine the ingredients together.

Once the peanut butter and coconut milk has combined, remove from the heat.

Squeeze the juice from your lime, and add the curry powder, sweet chilli sauce, agave syrup and salt and pepper into the creamy mixture.

Whisk until smooth, then transfer to a small bowl, cover and set aside until required (the longer you leave it, the more time the flavours will infuse together).

Carefully thread the chicken pieces through the wooden skewers, leaving some space at either end (don't forget that if you are using wooden skewers, soak them in cold water for about 30 minutes before adding the chicken to stop them from burning).

Place the skewers on a hot griddle pan for about 5-6 minutes each side, turning once. Double check that the chicken is cooked through, by testing one piece - you can always grill it for a little longer if necessary.

Serve with chopped raw onion, cucumber shreds, baby cos lettuce and the spicy peanut sauce and scattered crushed peanuts.

LISA'S TIP

Serve these straight from the griddle pan or chill to have at a picnic. These are fun to make with children and can also be cooked on a BBQ. Children always like 'food on a stick'!

Sesame Seared Tuna & Avocado Salsa

This dish has the look of one that has been professionally
prepared, but it is surprisingly easy!

{Serves 4-6}

ingredients

400g tuna loin
1 tbsp black sesame seeds
sea salt and cracked black pepper
1 tbsp white sesame seeds

salsa

2 avocados, chopped
1 red onion, finely chopped
4 medium tomatoes, de-seeded and chopped
2 tsp sweet chilli sauce
1 tbsp olive oil
sea salt and cracked black pepper

dressing

3 spring onions, finely chopped
2 garlic cloves, finely minced
1 lime, juice
2 tbsp fresh coriander
2 tbsp fish sauce
3 tsp palm sugar
2 tbsp honey, agave nectar or maple syrup
1 tbsp sweet chilli sauce

garnish

½ bag of rocket
1 lime, cut into wedges
tamari soy sauce, gluten-free

Preparation time - 60 mins, cooking time - 2 mins, chilling time - 5 to 6 hours or overnight

To make the seared tuna, place the sesame seeds in a shallow tray and season lightly with salt and black pepper. Wash and pat dry the tuna lightly with kitchen paper. Using your hands press the tuna into the seasoned sesame seed mixture on all sides. Heat a non-stick pan over a medium/high heat. When the pan is hot, sear the tuna for no longer than 20-30 seconds on each side to seal.

Take the fish off the heat and set aside to rest. When cooled, lay a sheet of cling film on a clean work surface and then lay another sheet of cling film over the top repeat until you have 4 or 5 layers. Put the tuna at one end of the cling film and roll up tightly to make a fat cigar shape, twist the ends tightly like a cracker (rolling the tuna tightly in cling film will ensure the fish has a good round shape for professional-looking, even slices)

Chill for 5-6 hours – ideally do this in the morning, ready to serve in the evening.

For the dressing, mix all the ingredients in a bowl, leave to stand and infuse.

To make the salsa, place the chopped avocado, finely chopped red onion and de-seeded tomatoes, in a bowl with the olive oil, sweet chilli sauce, sea salt and black pepper and toss together.

Half an hour before serving, remove the tuna from the fridge, discard the cling film, then thinly slice. Place equal numbers of slices on each plate. Garnish with avocado salsa in the centre topped with a handful of rocket on each place. Drizzle with dressing on each plate around the tuna, garnish with a lime wedge, serve with a side dish of soy sauce.

LISA'S TIP

*When you purchase your tuna (recommended to buy from a Japanese fishmonger), make sure your tuna is shaped like a loin and is bright red or dark pink. If it is maroon or brown, it is not sashimi grade, so it will not be a good candidate for this recipe. **Substitution:** Beef can be cooked the same way as tuna. For more well done, leave on for 60 seconds on each side.*

Pea Soup

A surprisingly simple but elegant soup.
A few sprigs of fresh dill also works well.

....

{Serves 4-6}

ingredients

1 tbsp olive oil

4 shallots, finely chopped

1 stick of celery, cut in half (will be discarded from the soup before blending)

1 chicken stock cube, gluten-free, dissolved in 570ml boiling water

1 vegetable stock cube, gluten-free, dissolved in 570ml of boiling water

1 kilo frozen peas (look for petit pois – the smaller ones)

sea salt and white pepper

garnish

drizzle olive oil

mint

pea shoots

Preparation time - 20 mins, cooking time - 20 mins

Finely chop the shallots and cut the celery stalk in half.

Place a saucepan on the stove with the olive oil, sauté the shallots until translucent. Add the celery stalk and season lightly with sea salt and white pepper.

Add the frozen peas and stir for about 2 minutes.

Dissolve the chicken and vegetable stock cubes in a little over a litre of boiling water. Pour into the saucepan, bring to the boil and reduce to a medium heat. Cook for 20 minutes.

Remove from the heat, discard the celery stalk and blend either in a liquidiser or with a hand held blender.

Place in individual serving bowls with a drizzle of olive oil for garnish and some pea shoots and mint.

LISA'S TIP

If you find that the soup is too thick after blending, pour in a little water to thin out the soup, alternatively you can pour the soup through a fine meshed sieve. You may also wish to freeze this soup, for a maximum of 2 -3 months.

Baked Asparagus in Parmesan & Almond Crust

Parmesan is lower in fat than many other cheeses plus its
robust flavour means that a little goes a long way.

{serves 4-6}

Ingredients

460g asparagus spears, thick
(approx. 15 spears), trimmed, with
bottom 2/3 of each spear peeled

2 large eggs, beaten

2 tsp honey mustard

80 ground almonds

80g parmesan cheese, finely grated

sea salt and white pepper

garlic granules

paprika

avocado dip

2 avocados

2 tsp lemon juice

4 tsp tahini

4 tsp cold water

sea salt and white pepper

Preparation time - 30 mins, cooking time - 20 to 25 mins

Preheat the oven to 425°F, gas mark 7, 220°C (200°C fan assisted).

Line a large baking tray with parchment paper or use a silicone baking mat.

Cut about 3cm off the bottom of each asparagus, then using a vegetable peeler, peel halfway down to the bottom of the spear all around the asparagus, this will eliminate most of the stringiness. It also looks and tastes better!

Place the ground almonds and grated parmesan on separate plates.

In a large oval dish, add the beaten eggs, honey mustard, and season with sea salt, white pepper, garlic granules and paprika.

Place one asparagus spear in the egg mixture then roll in the ground almonds, then place back in the egg mixture coating all around, then coat in the parmesan cheese.

When finished coating the asparagus, place on the lined baking tray and repeat this method with all the asparagus

If you have extra almond meal and parmesan, mix together and sprinkle over the asparagus on the tray.

Place the asparagus in the preheated oven, bake for 20-25 minutes, turning over after the first ten minutes and then keep turning over to ensure all sides are golden and crispy.

To make the dip, blend the avocado in a food processor until smooth and then add the lemon juice, tahini and water.

Season the dip with sea salt and white pepper and continue to blend until smooth. Check the seasoning and adjust if needed.

Serve with the avocado dip.

LISA'S TIP

Make sure the asparagus are not pencil thin. You need thick asparagus for this recipe. This recipe is suitable for an everyday snack or served as a healthy canapé. Asparagus' season is Spring and in the past I have stir-fried or blanched them. This recipe is easy to make and tastes great. Mmmm, delicious green asparagus dipped into creamy avocado, nutritious and delicious! Make sure you eat the crunchy bits which might be left on the tray - they're the best part!

Tomato Soup

A delicious and healthy soup that lends
itself to making big batches to use later.

{makes 2 litres}

ingredients

1.8kg tomatoes, cut in half
(combination of classic vine, plum,
cherry, Jack Hawkins)

4 enchalion shallots, sliced

2 celery stalks

2 carrots, cut into big batons

2 tbsp olive oil

1 tsp tomato purée

1-2 tsp honey, agave nectar or
maple syrup (depending on the
sweetness of the tomatoes, add 2nd
spoon if needed after the soup has
been liquidised)

2 tsp bouillon powder, gluten-free

1 litre boiling water

sea salt and black pepper

bouquet garni

garnish

75ml soy cream

2 slices gluten-free brown bread

olive oil

cracked black pepper

preparation time - 30 mins, cooking time - 40 mins

In a large saucepan add the olive oil and sauté the shallots until
translucent.

Add the tomatoes and continue to sauté for 5 minutes over a
medium heat.

Add the carrots, celery and tomato purée.

Season with sea salt and black pepper.

Add the bouquet garni and honey, agave nectar or maple syrup.

Dissolve the bouillon in the boiling water, then add to the tomatoes.

Bring back to a boil then simmer for 40 minutes.

Discard the celery and carrot before blending.

Blend the soup in a liquidiser in several batches.

Place the sieve over a large bowl and ladle the soup into the sieve.

Using the back of the ladle, push the pulp down into the bowl below.

Continue until all the soup has been sieved and transfer it back into
the pan, reheat if necessary. Discard the pulp.

To make the croutons, cut both slices of the bread into 1cm cubes,
drizzle with olive oil, sprinkle with sea salt and bake in the oven for
8-10 minutes on a medium heat until crisp and browned (watch
they don't burn!).

Taste and adjust seasoning as required.

Stir in the soy cream, sprinkle with black pepper and croutons,
and serve.

LISA'S TIP

*This is one yummy soup and surprisingly easy. Once you make this,
you'll never be able to go back to canned soups!! This soup improves
on the second day, though it's so good on the first day that there's
often not one drop left. Store it in the refrigerator for one day, or
freeze it for a couple of months.*

Cauliflower Egg Fried Rice

Ditch the take-away! This delicious dish is low on carbs but features all the flavours of the traditional Chinese dish, without the rice!

{Serves 4}

ingredients

1 large cauliflower (760g approx.), florets broken off

2 echalion shallots, finely chopped

150g frozen petit pois, thawed

3 large eggs, beaten

1 tsp sesame oil

1 tbsp coconut oil (virgin or odourless)

sea salt and white pepper

garnish

toasted sesame seeds

teriyaki or tamari soy sauce, gluten-free

Preparation time - 30 mins, cooking time - 20 mins

Break off the cauliflower florets, rinse in a colander and leave to dry completely.

Then place in a food processor until the cauliflower has broken down and you have a rice-like texture (don't over process or it will get too mushy).

In a mixing bowl, beat the eggs and season with sea salt and white pepper.

In a non-stick frying pan, add the sesame oil, heat and then add the eggs, scramble, then place on a plate when cooked.

In a clean non-stick frying pan, add the coconut oil, sauté the shallots until soft and translucent then season with sea salt and white pepper.

Add the ground cauliflower and cook for 5 minutes, then add the frozen peas and continue to cook for a further 5 minutes, check for seasoning.

Add the scrambled egg to the cauliflower and continue to cook.

You can add some teriyaki or tamari soy sauce at this point or leave for garnish.

LISA'S TIP

I LOVE fried rice, and often make my own fried rice at home with brown rice or quinoa which is delicious. But sometimes when I want to cut down on my carbs, I opt for cauliflower rice, an alternative to the typical grain. So tasty, simple and a wonderful way to eat cauliflower.

Crispy Curly Kale

For years this dish has been called 'fried seaweed' in Chinese restaurants.
It's so good, it's hard to believe it's good for you!

{Serves 4}

ingredients

200g curly kale, washed
1-2 tbsp olive oil
sea salt and black pepper
1 tsp coconut sugar

garnish

toasted sesame seeds
onion salad crispies (gluten-free)
½ tsp coconut sugar (if needed)

Preparation time - 5 mins, cooking time - 16 to 18 mins

Preheat the oven to 375°F, gas mark 5, 190°C (170°C fan-assisted).

Line a baking tray with parchment paper or silicone baking mat.

Place the curly kale on the baking tray and discard any hard stalks.

Drizzle with olive oil and lightly massage into the kale leaves.

Season with sea salt and black pepper.

Sprinkle with coconut sugar.

Bake in the pre heated oven for 16-18 minutes, stirring every 4-5 minutes.

When the leaves have gone crisp, remove from the oven.

Place in a serving bowl and garnish with toasted sesame seeds, coconut sugar (if needed) and onion salad crispies.

LISA'S TIP

Be sure to check the chips to make sure they don't burn. Kale is now being hailed as the 'queen of greens' since it's not only naturally low-calorie, it is also packed with Vitamins A and C; A which keeps the eyes healthy, and C, which hydrates the body and speeds up the metabolism. Kale also has powerful antioxidants, including flavonoids and carotenoids.

Lamb Shanks

Serve with creamy polenta or horseradish mashed potatoes. If you want a modern twist, you can also serve this dish on a bed of sautéed shallots and crushed edamame beans.

{Serves 4}

ingredients

4 lamb shanks x 275g each, washed and pat dry

250g button mushrooms, finely chopped

300g chantenay carrots, whole

2 small onions, peeled and finely chopped

6 shallots, peeled and leave whole

4 garlic cloves, minced

2 x 400g tins cherry tomatoes, sieved, pulp and seeds discarded

2 tbsp honey, agave nectar or maple syrup

3 tbsp olive oil

570ml chicken stock, gluten-free

50g cornflour

150ml red wine, full-bodied

2 tsp Worcestershire sauce, gluten-free

1 tbsp tomato paste

paprika

sea salt and cracked black pepper

garlic granules

Preparation time - 40 mins, cooking time - 2 ¾ hours

Preheat the oven to 350°F, gas mark 4, 180°C (160°C fan-assisted).

On a chopping board, sprinkle cornflour, paprika, sea salt, cracked black pepper and garlic granules and mix together.

Place each shank in the seasoned flour and coat all sides of the shank.

In a large casserole dish, heat the olive oil over a medium heat, place each shank in the casserole dish and brown very well on all sides, then remove from the dish.

In the casserole dish, add the finely chopped onions, mushrooms and garlic, stirring until onions are soft.

Then add the red wine, reduce for 5 minutes, then add the tomato paste.

Place a sieve over the casserole dish and squeeze through the tomato sauce, season with garlic granules, sea salt and cracked black pepper.

Add the Worcestershire sauce, shallots and carrots.

Return the lamb to the casserole dish, add the chicken stock, bring the liquid to the boil and add the honey.

Cover with a lid and transfer to the oven for 2¾ hours, turning the lamb shanks occasionally.

After 2 hours reduce the oven temperature to 300°F, gas mark 2, 150°C (130°C fan-assisted) and cook for a further 45 mins.

LISA'S TIP

I have to say I do love meat on the bone and there's something delightful about a braised lamb shank. When the meat is sweet, succulent and soft enough to scrape away with a fork it just can't be beaten. This is a dish I love to serve for family and friends at a dinner party. It's quite a comforting dish and is at its best when its spring lamb!

Asian Fish Stew

This rich, satisfying stew called 'laksa' is a lunchtime treat cooked in Asia's open air markets. To make the experience truly authentic, be sure to add the beansprouts and lime right before eating!

....

{Serves 4}

ingredients

800g firm, thick white fish fillets (haddock and cod) cut into 5-7cm pieces

250g gluten-free, sweet potato and buckwheat noodles

450ml fish or chicken stock, gluten-free

400ml organic coconut milk (canned)

2 tsp nam pla (Thai fish sauce)

½ tbsp lime juice

55g beansprouts

2 tsp palm sugar

sea salt

laksa paste

6 coriander stalks with leaves

3 large garlic cloves, crushed

1 red chilli, deseeded and chopped

1 lemon grass stalk, soft centre part only, chopped

3cm piece fresh ginger peeled and chopped

1 tbsp Worcestershire sauce, gluten-free

½ tsp turmeric

2 tbsp groundnut oil

garnish

lime wedges

fresh coriander

2 handfuls of beansprouts

Preparation time - 30 mins, cooking time - 50 to 60 mins

Put the fish or chicken stock in a saucepan over a high heat and slowly bring to the boil, then lower the heat and simmer for 10 minutes.

Make the laksa paste by putting all the remaining paste ingredients (except the oil) in a food processor and blend. Then with the motor running, slowly add up to 2 tbsp of oil until a paste forms.

Heat a large casserole dish adding the paste and stir-frying until it is fragrant. Now turn off the heat.

Stir the stock into the laksa paste, along with the coconut milk, nam pla, palm sugar and lime juice. Bring to the boil, then lower the heat, cover and simmer for 30 minutes.

Meanwhile, cook the noodles as directed on the packaging until soft, then run them under cold water. This washes off the starch and stops the cooking process. Drain and set aside in a colander.

Add the fish and beansprouts to the simmering laksa stew and continue cooking just until fish is cooked through, approx. 10 minutes.

Pour boiling water over the noodles to refresh them. Divide the noodles between four bowls and ladle the stew over, making sure everyone gets an equal share of the fish.

Garnish with the beansprouts, lime wedges and coriander.

LISA'S TIP

You can substitute the fish with chicken, tofu, mushrooms or combine them all. This is one of the most requested recipes for a get-together with my friends. Maybe it's because the sweet, sour, spicy, salty and savoury flavours of Asia are a fantastic way to fill a bowl and this is also an easy dish to make. Try potato & buckwheat, soba or black rice noodles for variety.

Sticky BBQ Chicken

This Sticky BBQ Chicken can be made year-round in the oven.
A crunchy salad complements this dish perfectly.

....

{Serves 4-6}

ingredients

8 x chicken thighs, skin-on and
bone-in

1 tbsp sesame oil

garlic granules

paprika

sea salt and white pepper

marinade

2 celery stalks, peeled (stringy
bits removed) and grated on a
microplane

2 enchalion shallots, grated on a
microplane

2 garlic cloves, crushed

1 tsp ginger minced

100ml tomato pasta sauce (a
smooth sauce is best)

50ml cold water

50ml tamari soy sauce, gluten-free

50ml mirin sweet rice vinegar

2 tsp American mustard

2 tsp sweet chili sauce

3 tsp honey, agave nectar or
maple syrup

½ lemon, juice

Preparation time - 40 mins, cooking time - 50 to 60 mins, marinade time - 10-15 minutes or overnight

Preheat the oven to 400°F, gas mark 6, 200°C, (180°C fan-assisted).

Mix all the ingredients for the marinade in a large mixing bowl (keep 100ml aside for heating up in a sauce pan to serve later).

Rub the sesame oil into the chicken thighs and season well with white pepper, garlic granules, sea salt and paprika.

Place the thighs in large sealable bags, spoon over some over the marinade to cover the thighs and let marinate for 10 – 15 minutes or preferably overnight.

When ready to cook, remove thighs and reserve marinade.

Transfer the chicken into a roasting tray with a couple of spoonfuls of marinade.

Place in the oven for about 50-60 minutes, turning occasionally and basting with the marinade and juices until thoroughly sticky and golden, adding extra marinade to the tray if necessary.

Start basting the thighs after 20 minutes and then baste 2 or 3 times for the duration of the cooking process.

They'll be done when they are nicely browned and the juices run clear when pierced with a knife (it's important you cook the chicken all the way through).

Heat reserved marinade in a small saucepan, reduce heat and simmer for 5 minutes.

Once the chicken pieces are cooked, eat them when fresh and hot. Just before serving, pour some extra sauce over them or leave to cool before packing up for a picnic or packed lunch.

LISA'S TIP

If you prefer, you can cook these thighs on the BBQ. Note that sauces with high sugar content will cause flare-ups when cooking over direct heat and may burn the chicken. Where possible apply BBQ sauce towards the end of the grilling time - just enough for the sauce to caramelize and crust on the chicken without burning. You can use the extra sauce to marinate lamb chops, too.

Shoulder of Lamb Baked with Rice

Sweet raisins and cinnamon give this
classic lamb dish a Greek twist.

{Serves 6-8}

ingredients

1kg shoulder of lamb, cubed

500g red rice, rinsed

500ml cold water

2 red onions, finely chopped

2 echalion shallots, finely chopped

150g puy lentils, ready-to-eat (pre cooked)

100g sultanas

350ml passata sauce

4 tbsp coconut oil (virgin or odourless)

2 garlic cloves, crushed

2 handfuls coriander, chopped

300ml almond milk

1 tbsp honey, agave nectar or maple syrup

sea salt, white and cracked black pepper

garlic granules

paprika

cinnamon

garnish

2 tbsp coconut oil (virgin or odourless)

2 onions, sliced

150g toasted cashew nuts

coriander

sea salt

Preparation time - 1 hour, cooking time - 2 hours

Preheat the oven to 400°F, gas mark 6, 200°C (180°C fan-assisted).

Rinse the red rice, then place in a saucepan with 500ml cold water, bring to boil then simmer for 30 minutes. Remove from heat, fluff with a fork and leave covered for a further 10 minutes. Place a large non-stick frying pan over a medium heat, add the cubed lamb and cook until you release all the juices.

Brown the lamb (you may need to pour away the juices every so often) this can take 5-10 minutes. In a large mixing bowl add: sea salt, white pepper, black pepper, garlic granules, paprika and cinnamon. Add the browned lamb to the mixing bowl, coat in the seasoning and leave to marinate for 10 minutes.

In a large 29cm oven-proof casserole dish add 2 tbsp coconut oil and sauté the shallots until soft, then add the cooked rice and continue to cook for 1 minute. Remove half of the rice mixture out of the casserole dish and set aside. With the back of a large spoon, smooth out the rice in the casserole dish on the base, and then spread equally 2 inches around the side of the dish. Set aside.

Add 1 tbsp coconut oil to a large non-stick frying pan, sauté the red onions until translucent, add garlic, coriander, puy lentils, sultanas, passata sauce and honey cook for further 10 minutes. Add the almond milk, bring to the boil, then simmer and add the lamb. Cook for 5 minutes. Carefully spoon the lamb and sauce into the prepared rice dish. Now evenly cover with the remaining rice and smooth out with the back of the spoon. Place in the preheated oven and cook covered for 1.5 hours.

For the last 30 minutes remove the lid and decrease the oven temperature to 350°F, gas mark 4, 180°C (160°C fan-assisted). In a small saucepan add 2 tbsp coconut oil and fry the sliced onions until crispy. Place on paper towel and sprinkle with sea salt. Roast the cashew nuts in the oven for 10-12 minutes until browned. When you're ready to serve, scatter onions, cashew nuts and coriander.

LISA'S TIP

This is a delicious one pot wonder dish. It's light, delicate and rich in flavours. It is perfectly accompanied by some chutneys and pickles and a light green salad.

Oven Baked Cod with Peppers & Olives

In Mediterranean coastal towns, the cuisine often combines the acidic flavour of tomatoes and fresh fish. With healthy dishes like this, no wonder their diet is considered the best!

....

{serves 4}

ingredients

4 x 200g cod fillets, skinless (middle pieces)
2 tbsp olive oil, plus extra for drizzling
1 garlic clove, crushed with salt to a puree
2 red onions, finely sliced
2 red peppers, skins removed, deseeded and thinly sliced
2 yellow peppers, skins removed, deseeded and thinly sliced
60g black olives, pitted (Nicoise or Kalamata)
2 tsp capers (optional)
sea salt and cracked black pepper

tomato sauce

1 box of baby tomatoes
4 shallots
2 garlic cloves
2 tbsp brandy (optional)
2 tsp tomato paste
400ml chicken or vegetable stock, gluten-free
1 tbsp honey, agave nectar or maple syrup
400g vine tomatoes, deseeded or you can use canned
1 bouquet garni (bay leaf, celery, thyme, leek) small pieces
50g coconut oil (virgin or odourless)
1 tbsp olive oil
mixed herbs
sea salt and cracked black pepper

garnish

fresh sprigs Greek basil
black pepper

Preparation time - 1 hour, cooking time - stove 30 mins, oven 8 to mins

To peel the peppers, place them whole under a preheated grill until they blacken, turning occasionally, about 10-12 minutes.

Remove from the grill, place in a large bowl and cover with cling wrap (or a food bag) until the peppers cool. Now deseed and thinly slice.

For the tomato sauce: slice the shallots, fry until soft with a little olive oil in a saucepan.

Add the chopped garlic, being careful not to burn the garlic, then add the tomato paste.

Cut the tomatoes in half and deseed, alternatively you may wish to use canned tomatoes. Add to the saucepan together with the baby tomatoes.

Add 200ml of chicken stock, turn the heat up until the sauce begins to boil, then reduce the temperature, season with sea salt and black pepper, add bouquet garni and a sprinkle of mixed herbs.

Slowly add the remaining stock, add cartouche (parchment paper pan lid with hole in the middle to let the steam out). Simmer slowly for 20 mins.

Pour the sauce ingredients through a fine sieve, return to stove on a low heat and gradually add honey, agave nectar or maple syrup and brandy. Slowly whisk in the coconut oil, then leave to the side.

Heat a little oil in a large heavy-based frying pan, add the red onions and sauté until soft about 6 minutes. Then add the garlic, olives and peppers, cook for a further 2 minutes seasoning lightly with a little salt and pepper. Add tomato sauce and capers, if using.

Preheat the oven to 375°F, gas mark 5, 190°C (170°C fan-assisted).

Warm sauce over a medium/heat.

In an oven proof dish pour in your tomato sauce, then add the cod to the ovenproof dish.

Cook for approximately 8-10 minutes.

Garnish with fresh springs of Greek basil or fresh oregano.

LISA'S TIP

If you are short for time you can skip the process of making your own tomato sauce and use a good quality smooth pasta sauce. You could serve this with some gluten-free bread or a side dish of either polenta, quinoa or brown rice.

Beef with Asparagus and Teriyaki Sauce

This is a lighter version than the one found in restaurants. There's no MSG or flour and the oil has been minimised. Try serving the dish with Cauliflower Fried Rice.

{serves 4}

ingredients

500g beef rump or sirloin steak, thinly sliced

1 large onion, thinly sliced

340g asparagus, trimmed, peeled and cut into 3 pieces diagonally

3 spring onions, cut into 3cm slices

2 garlic cloves, minced

1 tbsp palm sugar

2 tbsp teriyaki sauce, gluten-free

2 tbsp tamari soy sauce, gluten-free

1 tbsp water

1 tsp grated ginger

1 tsp sesame oil

2 tbsp groundnut oil

garnish

2 tbsp roasted cashew nuts

1 small chilli, sliced (optional for garnish)

bunch of fresh coriander

brown rice

Preparation time - 40 mins, cooking time - 15 to 20 mins

Prepare your asparagus by taking the root end off, and using a vegetable peeler, remove the top layer off around the asparagus 2.5cm from the bottom of the tip. Then cut into 3 pieces diagonally.

Now prepare your spring onions cutting them into 3cm slices.

Slice the beef in 1.5cm strips down the length of the piece of meat.

Heat half the oil in a wok, stir fry the beef in batches until browned, then remove to a plate to rest.

Mix the teriyaki sauce, tamari soy sauce, sugar and 1 tbsp water, then set aside.

Heat the remaining oil in the wok and stir fry the onion until soft and translucent, then add the asparagus and continue cooking for 10-12 minutes until al dente.

Return the beef to the wok with the garlic and ginger and cook for 30 seconds.

Add the spring onions, stir fry for 2 minutes, then add the sauce and cook for a further minute.

Scatter with cashew nuts and sliced chilli (optional) and garnish with coriander.

Serve immediately with steamed brown rice or gluten-free noodles.

LISA'S TIP

Asparagus - long regarded as one of the 'foods of love' is back! Asparagus is available from different parts of the world all year round but British asparagus is well worth waiting for – it has unbeatable flavour and freshness. The tips should be tightly furled and perky, rather than limp, and the shoots should be straight and firm.

Banana & Peanut Butter Ice Cream Cake

Both bananas and peanuts have positive health properties,
so here's a way of having your cake and eating it too!

{serves 8 - 10}

ingredients

200g crunchy granola bars, crushed

2 tbsp coconut oil, melted (virgin or odourless)

8 bananas, cut into 3cm pieces and put into the freezer

100ml soya single cream

4-6 tbsp crunchy peanut butter (if you prefer an intense peanut flavour)

garnish

50g dark chocolate, melted

Preparation time - 30 mins, freezing time - 6 to 8 hours or overnight for finished cake to set and time to pre-freeze banana chunks

Remove bananas from skins, cut into 3cm slices, place in a freezer bag and freeze overnight.

Line a 9 inch (23cm) loose bottomed, round cake tin with parchment paper.

Place the granola bars in a food processor and pulse until a sandy consistency.

Melt the coconut oil over a gentle heat, then add the crushed granola bars.

Place the granola mixture into the prepared tin, press firmly into the base and 3cm around the sides.

Place the banana slices in a food processor or powerful blender.

Purée banana slices, scraping down the bowl as needed.

Purée until the mixture is creamy and smooth, then add the soya single cream.

Add the crunchy peanut butter and purée to combine, then pour the mixture into the cake tin and freeze for 6-8 hours or overnight.

30 minutes before you are ready to serve, remove the ice cream cake from the freezer.

Melt the dark chocolate and drizzle over the cake.

Smile.

LISA'S TIP

If you are looking for a new way to use up your ripe bananas, try this Banana Peanut Butter Ice Cream cake. I always have loads of frozen banana chunks in my freezer, whether it's for a smoothie or this delicious cake. The recipe is super simple to make and no one will ever know there are only a few ingredients involved. This recipe really is magical and healthy too!

Lemon & Almond Cake

A fine textured cake which
is very rich – so small slices!

{serves 10}

ingredients

3 medium eggs

175g butter or margarine, room temperature

175g coconut sugar

100g fine cornmeal

1 tsp baking powder, gluten-free

175g ground almonds, sifted

1 unwaxed lemon, grated and freshly squeezed

½ tsp vanilla extract

drizzle

2 unwaxed lemons. grated and freshly squeezed

50g icing sugar

2 tbsp water

Preparation time - 30 mins, cooking time - 30 mins, cooling time 20 mins

Preheat the oven to 350°F, gas mark 4, 180°C (160°C fan-assisted).

Cream together the butter and sugar, add the eggs and vanilla extract and beat until roughly blended (do not over-beat as you do not want to incorporate too much air).

Add the fine cornmeal, baking powder and ground almonds. If you are using a food processor make sure you wipe the sides of the bowl during the mixing process. Add the juice and zest of one lemon and mix together until smooth.

Line the base and sides of a non-stick 20cm springform cake tin with parchment paper spoon the mixture in, level out and bake in the middle of the preheated oven for 30 minutes.

To make the syrup drizzle, place the lemon zest and juice in a small saucepan together with the icing sugar and water bring to a boil for 2-3 minutes then reduce to a simmer for 3 minutes to reduce the consistency to a syrup.

After 30 minutes remove the cake from the oven, let cool on a wire rack for 5 minutes.

Pierce the cake with a fine skewer or tooth pick making a about 20 small holes.

Pour the syrup through a sieve into a small bowl, the using a large spoon carefully spoon the syrup over the cake (keep the rind for garnish).

Loosen the springform tin and leave for 20 minutes while the cake absorbs the syrup.

Release the cake from the tin and serve.

LISA'S TIP

This recipe does have sugar and butter, although that's why it's in my treats section. I love the richness, moistness and lemony punch that this cake delivers! It is the ideal dessert for a glorious afternoon tea and would also make a scrummy pudding with a big dollop of frozen lemon curd sorbet!

Almond Macaroons

Different from macarons which are two lids with a filling, these macaroons
are the traditional ones made by grandmothers everywhere!

{Makes 20 macaroons}

ingredients

225g ground almonds
2 large egg whites only
115g coconut sugar
20 almonds, whole, blanched

Preparation time - 20 mins, cooking time - 18 to 20 mins

Preheat the oven to 325°F, gas mark 4, 180°C (160°C fan assisted)

In a large mixing bowl add the ground almonds and coconut sugar and mix well.

Gradually pour in the egg whites, then mix well to form a sticky mixture.

Pre-line a large baking tray with parchment paper or silicone baking mat.

Roll a heaped teaspoon of the almond mixture in the palm of your hands into a ball, (I wet my hands slightly to prevent too much sticking!) then place on the tray 4 rows of 5 spacing them evenly.

Dip your finger in a small bowl filled with cold water, flatten slightly then gently press into the macaroon and place a blanched almond in the middle.

Place in the pre-heated oven on the middle shelf for 18-20 minutes.

Allow to cool, then place on a wire rack to cool further.

LISA'S TIP

These are a great treat if you're following a gluten/dairy free diet! They are my grandma's special recipe and we make them together. The tip with macaroons is that they bake quickly and it's a judgement call as to when they are done enough. I actually prefer the pale ones which are soft throughout, although some people prefer a little colour and a harder shell. To be honest they taste great pale or slightly browned and if they are not eaten within a day (highly unlikely), they will get firmer in time so I would lean towards a light brown colour. They are great with a cup of tea or coffee any time!

Banana & Walnut Cake

A light textured cake with rich frosting – just make sure to have friends and family around so you can share!

....

{Serves 12 - 14}

ingredients

3 eggs, large
200ml rapeseed oil
3 bananas, mashed
225g coconut sugar, sifted
225g fine cornmeal (polenta), sifted
1 pinch sea salt
2 tsp baking powder, gluten-free
100g walnuts, broken up
100g sultanas

garnish

220g Philadelphia (or other full-fat) cream cheese
80g slightly salted butter
2 tsp custard powder
4 tbsp icing sugar
60g walnuts halves

Preparation time - 40 mins, cooking time - 55 mins, decorating time - 20 mins

Preheat the oven to 325°F, gas mark 3, 160°C, (140°C fan-assisted)

In a food mixer, or by hand, beat the eggs. Then add the sunflower oil.

In a large mixing bowl sift the sugars, cornmeal, baking powder and salt then add to the egg mixture. Beat until combined.

Fold in the mashed bananas, then add the broken walnuts and sultanas.

Line the base and sides of a non-stick 9in (23cm) spring form tin with parchment paper.

Pour in the mixture and bake on the middle shelf of the preheated oven for 55 minutes.

Remove from the oven when cooked and place on a cooling rack. After ten minutes, release the spring form tin and leave to cool.

To make the cream cheese frosting, beat by hand the cream cheese and butter until smooth. Add the custard powder and icing sugar.

When the cake is cooled, ice the cake, sides and top and decorate with walnut halves.

Remember to share!

LISA'S TIP

It truly is like banana bread in a fluffier form. Bananas have always been one of my favourite fruits for breakfasts and snacks and I love walnuts which are good for our brain and memory. So, I tried different experiments with both ingredients and the result is addictive! Bananas are packed full of goodness, including Vitamin C, potassium and dietary fibre. Any cake baked with them are my family's favourite, especially my grandma.

SUMMER

seasonal moods

Heat. Yes, even here. Where thoughts drift to recreating dishes we've had on holiday. Where we can stand outside and barbecue (even if we sometimes need an umbrella) fish or kebabs of fresh vegetables - all accompanied by giant salads with the rich red hues of tomatoes, brilliant gold of corn on the cob, creamy green of avocados, cucumbers and the more exotic edamame bean.

Then there are strawberries enjoyed on their own or with their seasonal friend, blueberries. Perhaps adding a dash of Middle Eastern mystery, dates.

It is an easy time to eat foods that are light and healthy. Choices are plentiful so get chopping.

AVOCADO Delicious and creamy, avocados provide nearly 20 essential nutrients, including fibre, potassium, vitamin E, B vitamins and folic acid.

CUCUMBER Containing more than 96% water and in the same family as melons and squashes, cucumbers are easily grown in many climates and are found in most global cuisines.

DATES Used in recipes instead of refined sugar, fresh dates should be plump and moist with glossy skins. Dried dates should still be glossy with an even colour.

STRAWBERRIES You may not realise that strawberries are actually part of the rose family and not technically a fruit. Low in sugar, they are ideal for people following a low-GI diet.

TOMATOES Forget oranges - tomatoes pack a mega punch when it comes to vitamin C. They also contain vitamin A, energy-boosting iron and potassium, which has been proven to reduce strokes.

BLACKBERRIES As well as tasting wonderful, blackberries are also rich in vitamins, minerals and antioxidants. They are also low in calories, carbohydrates and fat, making them one of the best fruits out there for a balanced diet.

BROCCOLI A close relative of cauliflower, and from the same family as cabbage and sprouts, broccoli has grown wild in the Mediterranean for hundreds of years.

EDAMAME BEANS Edamame are young soybeans usually still in the pod. The beans are picked when they are young and green ensuring they are soft and edible. Edamame are prized among vegetarians for their high protein content.

Berry & Oat Smoothie Bowl

People on gluten-free diets sometimes struggle at breakfast. Here's one solution that is a cross between oatmeal and a classic smoothie. Be sure to include the toppings for variety.

{serves 4-6}

Ingredients

500ml almond milk

160g frozen berries (strawberries, blueberries, raspberries and blackberries)

2 tsp honey, agave nectar or maple syrup (optional)

20g rolled oats, gluten-free

2 large bananas, fresh or frozen

garnish

banana chips, broken up

granola, gluten-free

blueberries

raspberries

blackberries

Preparation time - 20 mins, freezing fruits 6 - 8 hours

Peel and slice your bananas if not already frozen.

In a blender, combine the almond milk, bananas, frozen berries and agave nectar (or preferred choice).

Process until the mixture is smooth.

Add the oats and give a quick pulse.

Divide between two breakfast bowls and top with banana chips, granola, blueberries, raspberries and blackberries.

Enjoy with a clear conscience!

LISA'S TIP

This smoothie is perfect for a 'get up and go' morning. What's even better is that you can make it the night before and let it sit in the fridge. It will naturally thicken overnight that's why I like to serve it as a smoothie bowl rather than in a glass. For added fibre, I like to add some chia seeds or shredded toasted coconut, pecans, hemp seeds, cashew butter, fresh banana slices and strawberries and blueberries.

Freezing is the easiest and cheapest way to preserve fresh fruit and prevent food wastage. When I shop, I make sure to buy a good selection of fruit at different states of ripeness. I buy riper fruit to eat at the beginning of the week, and unripe fruit to eat later in the week. When I end up with too much ripe fruit at one time, I freeze the excess to use in smoothies and other foods!

Scrambled Eggs with Smoked Salmon & Avocado

Creamy scrambled eggs with flavourful salmon, a brunch
classic that also makes a quick and tasty dinner.

....

{serves 4}

Ingredients

10-12 large eggs, beaten (I like to
use 3 eggs per person, however you
can choose 2 per person)
sea salt and white pepper
2 tbsp rapeseed oil

garnish

2 avocados, sliced and
sea salt and black pepper
227g smoked salmon
chives
gluten-free wholemeal bread

Preparation time - 15 mins, cooking time - 3 to 5 mins

Break the eggs into a bowl and lightly beat them, season with sea
salt and white pepper.

Add the oil to a large non-stick pan on a high heat, then add the
eggs and reduce the heat to low.

Keep on the low heat, stirring continuously with a wooden spoon.
Continuously stirring over a low heat keeps the eggs nice and
creamy.

The eggs must remain soft and creamy, so keep an eye on them.

Always remove scrambled eggs from the heat when they are almost
set but still appear shiny and a bit underdone, as they carry on
cooking in the pan.

Take the scrambled eggs off the direct heat earlier if you are not yet
ready to serve (whilst toasting your bread).

Cut the avocados in half, make slices across the length. Scoop out of
the skin and season with sea salt and black pepper.

Just before serving you can chop up some chives for presentation
and serve with the smoked salmon and avocado.

Enjoy with friends.

LISA'S TIP

*Good scrambled eggs can be tricky to make because the mistake so
many people make is turning the heat up higher than necessary to
make them cook quicker. This will make them cook quicker – but it
will also make them rubbery. So be patient and always keep the heat
on medium/low, it is worth it for a decent result.*

Chia Seed & Granola Individual Breakfast Pots

By placing the mixture in Mason jars, you have now portioned for four breakfasts. Little things like this help to de-stress our lives.

....

{makes 4 individual pots}

Ingredients

500ml almond milk
8 tbsp chia seeds
2 tbsp agave nectar
240g granola, gluten-free
100g blueberries
100g raspberries
100g blackberries

garnish

4 strawberries
honey, agave nectar or maple syrup for drizzling

Preparation time - 30 mins, refrigeration 6 to 8 hours (overnight)

Pour 500ml almond milk into a measuring cup and add the agave nectar (or preferred choice) and chia seeds. Give it a mix and then ten minutes later give it another stir, cover with cling film and then leave either overnight or for at least a few hours.

Wash and pat dry your berries.

Remove the chia seed pudding from the refrigerator and give a gentle stir.

Using 4 Mason type jars with lids, layer the jars with chia seed pudding at the bottom then berries, then granola then repeat with chia seed pudding, berries and granola.

Garnish with strawberries and a drizzle of agave nectar (or preferred choice). Either eat straight away for a scrummy filling breakfast on the move (it travels well) or as a snack or dessert.

Keep in the refrigerator for 2 to 3 days once made.

Just as great with a variety of fruits!

LISA'S TIP

Now I love a good chia pudding, especially for breakfast or dessert. In fact anytime of the day! If you have your ear to the health-food ground, then you've heard of chia seeds, superfood extraordinaire. Packed with great things; full of fibre, healthy fatty acid omega 3, very high in protein and full of vitamins, these unassuming seeds are more than meet the eye.

Tomato & White Peach Salad

White peaches have a short season
so grab them when you see them!

{serves 4}

Ingredients

6 large tomatoes, skinned and deseeded

3 white peaches, each cut into 12
slices

125g goats cheese, soft & creamy

6 basil leaves, sliced thinly

1 handful chives, chopped

2 tbsp extra virgin olive oil

2 tbsp pine nuts, toasted

1 tbsp pumpkin seeds

sea salt and cracked black pepper

garnish

a few basil leaves scattered

red garnet micro herb

1-2 tsp agave nectar, honey or
maple syrup

Preparation time - 30 mins, cooking time - 5 mins

To remove skin from tomatoes, bring a large pan of water to the boil, and have a large bowl filled with ice cold water on the side. Cut a very shallow X on the top and bottom of the tomatoes and drop them into the boiling water 3 at a time. Using a slotted spoon, remove the tomatoes after 20-30 seconds and place into the prepared bowl of ice water. Let the tomatoes sit at least 5 minutes.

Once the tomatoes have been chilled, remove, then peel. If the skin is stubborn, use a small sharp paring knife being careful not to squeeze the tomato. Once skinned cut each tomato into quarters, then use a small knife or a teaspoon and scoop the seeds out. Now cut each quarter in half and place in a large mixing bowl. Season with sea salt and black pepper. Add extra virgin olive oil, chopped chives and sliced basil and mix well.

Remove the peach stone but cutting the peach in half and then cut each half into 6 slices. Add to the tomatoes.

Toast the pine nuts in a non-stick dry frying pan over a medium heat, keep shaking to prevent burning, place in a small bowl and add the pumpkin seeds.

To serve, place the tomatoes and peaches on a large platter, scatter the pine nuts, pumpkin seeds, and goats cheese. Drizzle the agave nectar (or preferred choice), garnish with basil sprigs and red garnet microherb.

LISA'S TIP

Savoury peach dishes aren't usually the first to come to mind but they are a fruit that goes beautifully with many cheeses and herbs.

Avocado, Cherry Tomato & Pine Nut Salad

Chock full of fresh herbs, this easily composed salad is
made special by the addition of pine nuts.

{serves 4 -6}

Ingredients

440g cherry tomatoes, cut in half
220g fine beans, trimmed
35g pine nuts, toasted
1 bunch coriander, finely chopped
1 bunch mint, finely chopped
1 bundle chives, finely chopped
2 avocados, each half sliced into 5
3 tbsp extra virgin olive oil
½ tbsp lemon juice
sea salt and cracked black pepper

garnish

fresh coriander
balsamic glaze

Preparation time - 20 mins, cooking time - 5 mins

Place the beans into boiling salted water and cook for 5 minutes. Then immediately place in a sieve and run under cold water to stop the cooking process. Now chop the beans finely.

Toast the pine nuts in a dry pan for 3-5 minutes, continually shaking the pan to prevent burning.

In large mixing bowl add: the cherry tomatoes which have been cut in half, chopped herbs, pine nuts and green beans. Toss well.

In a small bowl, mix the olive oil and lemon juice and season with sea salt and black pepper. Pour over the tomatoes.

Place the salad on your serving plates.

Then carefully place the sliced avocado over the salad.

Check for seasoning, garnish with balsamic glaze and coriander.

LISA'S TIP

This salad is simple and delicious. It's a great way to make use of the summer bounty of tomatoes. Enjoy as a starter or side dish or copy me and eat it as your main meal. This salad is packed with nutrition. It complements fish, meat and poultry if serving as a side dish.

Lemon and Rosemary Chicken

Easy to prepare and bursting with citrus flavour.
Serve with Pan-Fried Jersey Royal Potatoes.

....

{serves 4}

Ingredients

4 chicken breasts (supreme on the
bone with skin)
2 whole garlic bulbs
1 lemon, large, sliced
2-3 tbsp olive oil
garlic granules
2 stalks of rosemary
sea salt and cracked black pepper

Preparation time - 30 mins, cooking time - 40 mins (If you have time
you can marinate for 2 hours or overnight)

Pre-heat the oven to 350°F, gas mark 4, 180°C (160°C fan-assisted).

Place the chicken breast in a hot frying pan with a little olive oil
to seal the chicken, 2 minutes each side until the skin is crisp and
golden, then place in your roasting dish.

Cut both garlic bulbs in half, then rub all over the chicken breast
and place in the middle of the roasting dish.

Season with sea salt, black pepper and garlic granules on either side.

Slice your lemon into 6 slices and place over the chicken, then
squeeze each of the ends over the chicken.

Scatter 2 stalks of rosemary around the baking dish. Don't worry
about the rosemary sticking to the chicken, it tastes great when it's
cooked.

Pour a generous amount of olive oil - around 2 tablespoons - over
the chicken.

Place in the oven for 40 minutes, turning over after the first 20
minutes, start with the skin side down.

Cut your chicken breast in half on the diagonal when serving.

LISA'S TIP

*These chicken breasts are full of flavour and simple, yet fancy enough
for your next summer garden party. Grilled chicken breast is one
of my favourites. It is lean, tender and juicy. I love how the lemon
slices caramelizes during the cooking and becomes sweeter.*

Red Quinoa & Greek Feta Salad

Adding red quinoa to this Greek inspired salad makes the dish a more substantial one – meaning less desire to snack in the afternoon!

{serves 4}

Ingredients

250g red quinoa, rinsed

350ml cold water

1 large cucumber, peeled, deseeded and cut in small slices

250g medium size tomatoes, deseeded and cut in half or quarters

200g feta cheese, crumbled

60g Kalamata or green, olives sliced in half lengthways

¼ red onion, finely chopped

sea salt or herbamare and cracked black pepper

dressing

60ml extra virgin olive oil

4 tsp sushi seasoning vinegar

2 tsp Dijon honey mustard

2 tsp balsamic vinegar

garnish

fresh mint

Preparation time - 40 mins, cooking time - 30 mins

Place the quinoa in a sieve and rinse under cold running water, drain and then place in a medium-size saucepan with 350ml cold water. Bring to a boil then simmer for 20 minutes with the lid on.

After 20 minutes, remove from the heat, carefully fluff with a fork and leave to stand for ten minutes. Then place on a large plate to cool.

Remove the skin of the cucumber with a vegetable peeler. Cut down the length in half then each half again, then run the blade of your knife under the base of the seeds down the length of the cucumber, removing them.

Slice each quarter of the cucumber into smaller slices, then place in a large mixing bowl.

Cut the tomatoes in half, remove the seeds then cut in half again, add to the mixing bowl.

Add the sliced olives and red onion to the cucumber and tomatoes and season well with sea salt and black pepper.

In a separate bowl, make the dressing by whisking the olive oil, Dijon honey mustard, sushi seasoning and balsamic vinegar.

Fold the cooled red quinoa into the salad, toss, then drizzle over the dressing.

Add the crumbled feta and check for seasoning.

Garnish with fresh mint and serve.

LISA'S TIP

Just before serving I like to add in some avocado, to give a little creamy texture, you can also add some sundried tomatoes, or artichokes. For those who do not know, quinoa is a type of edible seed that originated in the Andes of South America. Quinoa is pronounced "keen-wah" and not "key-nowah" like I first thought!

Seared Steak, White & Green Bean Salad

Will convert even the most stalwart of 'meat and potatoes' men!
My father has just asked for me to make it again!

{serves 4-6}

Ingredients

4 sirloin or rib eye steaks

300g cherry tomatoes, cut in half (combination of yellow and red cherry tomatoes)

300g French green beans, blanched

4 large tomatoes, skinned & de-seeded

410g white butter beans, tinned, rinsed and drained

1 tbsp olive oil

sea salt and cracked black pepper

garlic granules

paprika

dressing

2 shallots, finely chopped

2 handfuls basil, chopped

2 handfuls coriander, chopped

2 tbsp sushi seasoning vinegar

1 tbsp sweet chilli sauce

100ml extra virgin olive oil, plus 2 tbsp olive oil for frying shallots

1 tsp agave nectar, honey or maple syrup

2 garlic cloves

garnish

½ red onion, sliced

crispy fried onions, salad toppers (gluten-free)

Preparation time - 40 mins, cooking time - 10 mins

Cook the French green beans in slightly salted water for 4-5 minutes, take out using a slotted spoon (retaining salted water on the stove), immerse beans in cold water to stop the cooking process, then drain.

Using the same water as above make a cross incision on the top of the large tomatoes, then place in the boiling water for 2 minutes and then into cold water to remove the skins. When cooled, cut into quarters and deseed then cut into strips.

Drain the butter beans through a sieve and place in a large mixing bowl, add the cherry tomatoes, larger tomato strips and green beans.

To make the dressing, finely chop the shallots, fry in 2 tbsp olive oil until sautéed and then add the garlic. Season with sea salt and black pepper.

Place the shallots and garlic in a mixing bowl and leave to cool.

In a mini chopper, place the cooled shallots and garlic, the remaining olive oil, vinegar, sweet chilli sauce, agave nectar (or preferred choice) and chopped herbs. Blend and then taste for seasoning.

Pour half of this dressing in the bowl with the tomatoes and beans. Toss then place on a flat serving platter.

Season the steaks on both sides with sea salt, black pepper, garlic granules and paprika.

Heat a non-stick frying pan with 1 tbsp olive oil, cook the steaks over a medium/high heat for 2-3 minutes per side or until cooked to your liking.

Remove, place on a plate and leave to rest (the steaks will continue cooking while resting, so don't overcook if you like it pink).

Slice the steak into equal size strips, and place over the beans and tomatoes.

Drizzle with the remaining dressing.

Garnish with the sliced red onion and crispy fried onions.

LISA'S TIP

This delicious steak salad has a fiesta of flavours, for a quick and tasty family friendly weeknight meal. I am currently in tomato heaven! Tomatoes are in season and I am love, love, loving them! Tomatoes combined with the hearty white and French green beans and tossed with this mouthwatering dressing, it's a knockout combination.

Quinoa Salmon & Avocado Sushi

Don't worry if your first sushi rolls
aren't perfect – it takes practice!

....

{serves 4}

Ingredients

250g quinoa, rinsed

450ml cold water

250g salmon, strips (as fresh as
possible, best to get from fish
counter and ask for sashimi grade)

5 tbsp sushi seasoning vinegar

7 sheets of nori seaweed

1 avocado, sliced lengthways into
14 strips

handful chives

3 tbsp mayonnaise

sesame seeds, toasted

garnish

tamari soy sauce or teriyaki,
gluten-free

pickled ginger

wasabi

Preparation time - 1 to 2 hours, cooking time - 20 mins

Place the quinoa in a fine sieve and rinse under cold water until the water runs clear (not cloudy), then leave the quinoa to drain through a strainer for around 30 minutes.

Add the quinoa to a saucepan with 450ml cold water. Bring to the boil, then cover and simmer on a low heat for 20 minutes.

Remove from the heat and carefully fluff with a fork, then leave to settle for 10 minutes with the lid on.

Pour the quinoa onto a large platter and coat all the grains with sushi seasoning vinegar. Then quickly cool down the quinoa, you can use a fan or magazine!

The quinoa will become glossy as it absorbs the vinegar mixture, do not over stir as it will become mushy.

Cover with a damp cloth while making the sushi variations (Quinoa will keep up to 3 hours at room temperature. Do not refrigerate).

Prepare your fillings: salmon, avocado and chives.

Cover a bamboo rolling mat in cling film, wrapping over a couple of times.

Fill a small bowl with water for sealing the edges of the nori sheets.

Place your rolling mat in front of you, cut off two sections from the top of the seaweed sheet (you will see an indentation) then place on to the rolling mat shiny-side facing down about 2cm from the edge.

Divide the quinoa into 7 parts, so you have enough for each roll.

Take 1 part of quinoa and place on the prepared seaweed sheet. Spread the quinoa evenly, leaving 1cm margin at the top uncovered. Flatten the quinoa and make sure it's neat at the edges.

Place the mayonnaise 2cm from the closest part of the seaweed towards you along the width. Then place your fillings. Do not overload. You can also sprinkle some sesame seeds.

Lift the near edge of the rolling mat and fold it over the filling (holding the filling in place with your middle and forefingers,

LISA'S TIP

Cover a bamboo rolling mat in cling film, wrapping over a couple of times, to prevent your fillings getting caught in the mat. This way it keeps your mat nice and clean.

aiming to meet the top edge of the quinoa, roll over approx. 3 times.

Lift the mat slightly to uncover the roll and remove your fingers from inside the roll, continue to roll until the two edges of the nori sheet meet.

Dip your fingertip in the water bowl and seal the top of the nori sheet.

Cover the roll with the rolling mat again and gently press along the length a couple of times, before removing the mat.

Place the rolls to the side until you have finished rolling, then using a serrated sharp knife, (and wiping the blade with a damp cloth to stop the quinoa from sticking) cut in the centre, then each half in two!

Asian Chicken Salad

This colourful, crunchy, tangy salad can be served at a picnic or
simply when you have leftover chicken or turkey!

{serves 4 - 6}

Ingredients

1 whole cooked chicken, deboned
and shredded

400g shredded white, red or
Chinese cabbage

4 tsp sesame oil

1 tsp tamari soy sauce, gluten-free

4 tbsp teriyaki sauce, gluten-free

6 tbsp sushi seasoning (sweet
vinegar)

1 avocado, blended in a food
processor until smooth

sea salt and cracked black pepper

garnish

1 handful chives, finely chopped

2 tbsp sesame seeds, toasted

2 tbsp cashew nuts, toasted

fresh coriander, roughly chopped

chilli flakes

Preparation time - 30 mins

Remove the skin from the pre-cooked chicken, debone and shred
the white/dark meat. Place the meat in a large bowl.

Add the sesame oil, tamari soy sauce and teriyaki to the shredded
chicken. Mix well then add the avocado.

Toast the sesame seeds in a dry frying pan on a gentle heat until
golden. Remove the seeds from the heat and leave to cool.

In another large mixing bowl, add the shredded cabbage together
with sushi seasoning (sweet vinegar).

Add your seasoned shredded chicken into the cabbage mixture
and toss.

Using a pair of kitchen scissors, cut the chives over the salad bowl.
Add the roughly chopped coriander.

Check for seasoning and add sea salt and black pepper to taste.

Garnish with the toasted sesame seeds, toasted cashew nuts and
chilli flakes.

LISA'S TIP

*The heat of summer calls for grilling and quickly prepared salads.
Once you have mastered this salad, you may like to vary it by adding
some chili, shredded carrots, mango or mint.*

Moroccan Beef Parcels with Hummus

Gently spiced beef served over creamy hummus and crunchy lettuce.
Wonderful textures and exotic seasoning.

....

{serves 4 - 6}

Ingredients

500g lean mince beef

2 enchalion shallots, finely chopped

30g pine nuts, toasted

2 tsp onion soup mix, gluten-free

2 tsp honey, agave nectar or maple syrup

1 tbsp rapeseed oil

garlic granules

ground cinnamon

sea salt and cracked black pepper

garnish

4 tbsp tahini

4 tbsp water

⅔ tsp lemon juice

handful coriander

250g hummus (make your own or shop bought)

4-6 baby gem lettuce, separate the leaves, to serve

chilli flakes

sea salt and white pepper

Preparation time - 40 mins, cooking time - 40 mins

In a non-stick frying pan, toast the pine nuts until lightly browned, then remove and place on a plate to cool.

Add 2 tbsp rapeseed oil, fry the shallots until translucent.

Now add the lean mince beef and continue to stir until the meat is browned, about 5 minutes, over a medium heat.

Season generously with sea salt, black pepper, garlic granules, ground cinnamon and onion soup powder mix.

Continue back on the heat for a further 5 minutes, then add the honey (or preferred choice) and chopped fresh coriander.

Add the toasted pine nuts, cook for a further 5 minutes on a low heat, then leave to cool.

Add the tahini, water, lemon juice, chopped coriander to a mini food chopper and blend together then season and check for consistency.

When you are ready to serve, place the beef mixture in a sharing bowl, place hummus in the base of the baby gem lettuces, then fill with the beef mixture and drizzle a little tahini over the top and sprinkle with chilli flakes.

LISA'S TIP

In the summer, dishes that combine warm meats and crunchy leaves are most welcome. The creamy texture of hummus adds to this dish. Consider it a healthier version of a fully loaded burger (and tastier, too!).

Quinoa with Sautéed Leeks, Peas & Avocado

A summertime salad balancing soft
sautéed leeks and crunchy seeds.

{serves 4 - 6}

Ingredients

300g quinoa, rinsed
400ml cold water
3 leeks, sliced thinly
250g petit pois (frozen peas)
2 avocados, cubed
2 tbsp olive oil
60g pumpkin seeds
sea salt and white pepper
garlic granules

dressing

60ml olive oil
60ml apple juice
2 tsp honey mustard
2 tsp honey, agave nectar or
maple syrup
2 tbsp sushi seasoning vinegar
fresh coriander, bunch of coriander
fresh mint, small bunch
sesame seeds, toasted

Preparation time - 40 mins, cooking time - 15 to 20 mins

Rinse the uncooked quinoa through a sieve with cold water for 2 minutes, then drain well.

Place the quinoa in a medium saucepan with 400ml cold water bring to a boil, cover and simmer on a low heat for 20 minutes.

Remove from heat, carefully fluff with a fork cover and stand for 5 minutes, then spread onto a large flat platter to cool.

In a large non-stick frying pan add the oil, sauté the sliced leeks until translucent and soft, season with sea salt, white pepper and garlic granules.

Add the frozen peas to the sautéed leeks and continue to cook for 5 minutes, then remove from heat to cool.

Add the sautéed leeks and peas to the cooked quinoa, then add the pumpkin seeds.

In a measuring jug, add the olive oil, apple juice, honey mustard, agave nectar (or preferred choice), sushi seasoning vinegar, season with sea salt and black pepper.

Add the chopped mint, coriander and toasted sesame seeds.

When the salad is completely cooled, add the cubed chunks of avocado, mix through the salad then pour over the dressing.

LISA'S TIP

Picnic season is here. This quinoa salad is perfect for such an occasion, or really any summer night - it's light but satisfying, packed with plant based protein and packs well for dining al fresco.

Carrot & Courgette Soup

Carrot soup is surprisingly tasty and the addition of
leeks elevate it to a more sophisticated level.

{serves 4 - 6}

Ingredients

1.3kg carrots, cubed
680g courgettes, sliced
2 large echalions shallots, sliced
1 celery stalk, cut in half
1 bay leaf
1 leek finely sliced
1 ¼ litre boiling water
2 tbsp olive oil
2 tbsp tomato purée
2 tbsp bouillon powder, gluten-free
1 tsp coconut sugar
sea salt and white pepper

garnish

chives, finely chopped
150g vegetable crisps
drizzle of olive oil

Preparation time - 30 mins, cooking time - 40 mins

In a large saucepan over medium heat, sauté the shallots in olive oil until translucent, approx. 5 minutes.

Add the sliced leeks and sauté for 3 minutes with the onions.

Add the cubed carrots, continue to sauté for 3 minutes then add the courgettes.

Season with sea salt and white pepper.

Add the tomato paste and coconut sugar, stir until the vegetables are coated.

Add your bouillon powder together with the boiling water. Add the celery stalks and bay leaf then bring back to a boil for 3-5 minutes.

Reduce the heat to medium and cook for 40 minutes (if you find there is a lot of broth on the top, using a large spoon you can skim that off).

Remove from the heat and cool slightly. Discard the celery stalk.

Using a hand held blender, purée the soup in the pot, or purée in batches in a blender or food processor.

If the soup is too thick, add a little extra boiling water (almond or soya milk are also good choices).

Garnish with vegetable crisps, a drizzle of olive oil and finely chopped chives.

LISA'S TIP

Did you know that if you eat a bowl of vegetable soup, you will feel full for a longer period of time than if you drink a glass of water and eat the vegetables separately. Your body and brain actually recognize water differently when it's combined with food. So get smart and eat soup often to help control your appetite. This soup also contains low-to-medium glycaemic index (GI) ingredients, is low in fat and contains a good source of dietary fibre.

Cucumber & Dill Salad

Cool and refreshingly different with
the addition of sushi seasoning.

....

{serves 4}

Ingredients

2 large cucumbers, peeled, halved
and then sliced

2 tsp lemon juice

1 tsp sesame oil

4 tbsp sushi seasoning vinegar

2 tsp sweet chilli sauce

1 tsp honey, agave nectar or
maple syrup

1 handful dill, chopped

1 handful mint, chopped

1 handful chives, chopped

1 tbsp toasted sesame seeds

sea salt and white pepper

garnish

1 tbsp sesame seeds, toasted

Preparation time - 30 mins

Peel each cucumber, then cut them in half down the length, scoop
out the seeds with a teaspoon then slice down the length of both
halves of the cucumber and place in a large mixing bowl.

Finely chop the mint, dill, chives and place in the bowl with the
cucumbers and season with white pepper and a little sea salt.

In a separate small mixing bowl, add the lemon juice, sweet chilli,
vinegar, sesame oil and agave nectar (or preferred choice). Mix well
then pour over the cucumbers.

Sprinkle with toasted sesame seeds.

LISA'S TIP

*For me, cucumbers mean summer is almost here and I will be able
to slice, dice and chop fresh cucumbers into dishes of all shapes and
forms. Clearly I love all things 'cucumbery' – who doesn't? This salad
was inspired by those thinly sliced cucumbers marinated in rice
vinegar that are sometimes served with sushi. This is a refreshing
salad that is perfect for days when it's really scorching outside.*

Pan Fried New Potatoes with Shallots

This dish is a true celebration of the season as Jersey Royals are only available for a short-time. Substitute new potatoes if you want a year-round dish!

{serves 4-6}

Ingredients

750g Jersey Royals or new potatoes
5g rosemary sprigs
4 garlic cloves, crushed
4 Echalion shallots, cut in half
2-3 tbsp olive oil
sea salt and cracked black pepper

Preparation time - 30 mins, cooking time - 40 mins

Wash potatoes to remove any excess dirt.

Bring a large pan of water to the boil, add potatoes, bring back to the boil, then simmer gently for 15-20 minutes or until soft. Drain then run under cold water.

Remove the skins of the shallots, cut in half and then in a large non-stick frying pan, gently fry in the olive oil for 5 minutes until soft and set aside. Cut the potatoes in half lengthways then place them in the large non-stick frying pan with the shallots and put the pan back on the stove for a further 5 minutes.

Add another tbsp olive oil and season with sea salt, black pepper and crushed garlic

Add the rosemary sprigs to the frying pan, continue shaking the pan over the heat, to ensure that you get the potatoes crispy.

Serve hot or cold.

LISA'S TIP

Do not peel Jersey potatoes. Simply rub any flaky skin gently from the surface. Always put into boiling salted water - to seal in the flavour. Jersey Royal potatoes are the crème de la crème of the potato world and they have a unique sweet buttery flavour and melt-in-the-mouth texture.

Gazpacho Soup

This cold soup comes from the southern part of Spain, Andalucia, where summer temperatures can reach over 100°F! If you choose to make a very smooth version of this soup, be sure to add a crunchy garnish for contrast.

{serves 4}

Ingredients

10 large Jack Hawkins (or large beef) tomatoes, skins removed

2 ½ large cucumbers peeled and deseeded

1 small red onion

2 garlic cloves, minced

500ml V8 vegetable juice

4 tbsp sweet chilli sauce

4 tbsp white wine vinegar

2 tsp honey, agave nectar or maple syrup

4 tbsp mayonnaise or 1 avocado

salt & white pepper

garnish

2 large cucumbers peeled, deseeded and finely chopped

4 medium tomatoes, deseeded and finely chopped

5 slices of wholemeal gluten-free bread

1 red onion, finely chopped

olive oil

sea salt

Preparation time - 30 mins, cooking time - 10 to 12 mins, chilling time 2 to 3 hours or overnight

Preheat the oven to 400°F, gas mark 6, 200°C (180°C fan-assisted).

To remove the skins from your tomatoes, make a criss-cross incision on the top and place in a pot of boiling water for 1 minute. Then immediately immerse in cold water to stop the cooking process. The skin will now come away easily.

Cut the skinned tomatoes into quarters and place in a large mixing bowl.

Using a vegetable peeler, peel 2 ½ large cucumbers and deseed then cut into chunks and place in the mixing bowl with the tomatoes.

Cut the red onion into quarters and place in the mixing bowl.

Crush the garlic cloves.

Blend the tomatoes, cucumber, red onion and garlic together with the bottle of V8 juice in batches.

Pass the ingredients through a fine sieve and discard any pulp.

Then add sweet chilli sauce, white wine vinegar, mayonnaise (or avocado) and 2 tsp of agave nectar (or preferred choice), stir well.

Then add sea salt and pepper, then sieve again for a second time and stir well. Refrigerate for 45 minutes or overnight is best.

To make the croutons, remove the crust from all sides then cut length ways into 4 strips, then cut each strip into 7 small equal pieces, cut each piece in half again.

Place the croutons on a non-stick baking tray with a good drizzle of olive oil and a sprinkle of sea salt.

Place in the oven on a baking tray on a medium heat for 10-12 minutes. Keep an eye on the croutons and shake the tray after the first 5 minutes.

When the croutons are a nice golden colour, remove from the oven, and leave to cool.

Garnish with finely chopped tomatoes, cucumber, red onion, croutons and a drizzle of olive oil.

LISA'S TIP

This soup can be made the day before serving making it ideal for dinner parties or lazy weekends. If serving adults, a small shot of vodka is a wonderful addition. Note: the soup will keep up to 3 days refrigerated.

Artichoke, Edamame Bean & Potato Salad

A deliciously different summertime salad
that can be served hot or cold.

{serves 4 - 6}

Ingredients

400g artichoke bottoms (frozen)
200g edamame beans, (frozen or fresh), cooked and peeled
500g potatoes, cut into 2cm cubes
6 tbsp olive oil
sea salt and white pepper

garnish

1 lemon, ½ sliced, ½ juice
large handful of dill, chopped

Preparation time - 40 mins, cooking Time - 20 mins

Bring a large pan of salted water to the boil. Add the frozen artichoke bottoms and cook for approx. 15-20 minutes covered then drain.

Place the cubed potatoes in cold water. Bring to the boil and cook for 8 minutes, then drain under cold water.

Blanch the edamame beans in salted boiling water for 5 minutes. Drain, then place in a bowl filled with cold water and remove the bean husk.

Add 2 tbsp olive oil to a large non stick frying pan, add the cubed potatoes and cook for 5 minutes.

Add the edamame beans, season with sea salt and white pepper and cook for further 2-3 minutes.

Cut the artichoke bottoms in quarters or halves, depending on the size, add to the frying pan, with the remaining 4 tbsp olive oil and cook for further 5 minutes, add more seasonings if required.

Add the chopped dill and lemon juice, and lemon slices.

Either serve this salad warm or cold.

LISA'S TIP

This light and delicious summer salad combines zesty artichoke hearts with tender edamame beans. Artichokes, high in antioxidants and fibre, the flesh of these little beauties have a creamy flavour and texture despite their armoured exterior. I sometimes like to serve this salad with large shavings of parmesan cheese. Alternatively, this complements my Lamb Chops with Coriander & Mint.

Chicken & Cashews with Broccoli

A lighter, healthier version of
the Chinese takeaway treat.

....

{serves 4}

Ingredients

500g chicken breast fillets, sliced thinly

2 tbsp peanut oil or rapeseed oil

1 tsp sesame oil

1 garlic clove, minced

1 small leek, sliced thinly

1 red onion, sliced thinly

1 medium carrot, sliced thinly

250g broccoli, chopped coarsely

1 tsp cornflour

125ml chicken stock, gluten-free

3 tbsp teriyaki sauce, gluten-free

sea salt and cracked black pepper

garnish

75g unsalted roasted cashews

fresh coriander

sesame seeds, toasted

250g black gluten-free noodles or brown rice

Preparation time - 30 mins, cooking Time - 30 mins

Season the thinly sliced chicken pieces with salt and black pepper.

Heat half of the peanut or rapeseed oil with the sesame oil in a wok or a large frying pan. Stir fry the chicken in batches, depending on the size of your pan, until browned, for around 2-3 minutes, with a splash of teriyaki sauce. Now set aside.

Heat the remaining peanut oil in the wok, stir fry the red onion, garlic, leek, carrot and broccoli until the leek is soft. Add the carrot and broccoli and cook for 5 minutes.

Pour boiling water into your measuring jug with half a chicken stock cube, then mix in your cornflour.

Return the chicken to the wok with the chicken stock and teriyaki sauce. Stir and check for taste, seasoning if necessary.

Stir fry for about 8 minutes, then sprinkle with the roasted cashew nuts, toasted sesame seeds and fresh coriander.

Serve with your choice of brown rice or gluten-free noodles.

LISA'S TIP

Check that you have all the ingredients you need ahead of time. Make sure all the food is cut according to directions before you start. Never try to prepare food while stir-frying and be sure to cut all the ingredients the same size. Pre-heat the wok on medium-high heat for at least a minute before adding oil.

Thai Seared Beef & Mushroom Salad

Good quality meat is a must for
this quickly prepared dish.

{serves 4 - 6}

Ingredients

500g fillet steak or rib eye, cut into portions, or as a loin

2 tbsp coconut oil (virgin or odourless)

150g oyster mushrooms, sliced

150g shiitake mushrooms, stems removed and sliced

1 tbsp honey, agave nectar or maple syrup

1 tbsp tamari soy sauce, gluten-free

dressing

3 spring onions, finely chopped

2 garlic cloves, finely minced

1 lime, juice

2 tbsp fresh coriander, chopped

2 tbsp fish sauce

3 tsp palm sugar

2 tbsp honey, agave nectar or maple syrup

1 tbsp sweet chilli sauce

garnish

1 romaine lettuce

1 whole cucumber, deseeded and cut into thin strips

175g cherry tomatoes

2 tbsp sesame seeds

1 large handful of coriander

1 handful roughly chopped roasted peanuts

Preparation time - 30 mins, cooking Time 8 to 15 mins

Place a large non-stick frying pan on the stove, place the steak in the pan and seal each side for 2-4 minutes or until done to your liking. In total cooking times are as follows: (6-8 minutes for rare; 7-10 for medium-rare; 10-12 minutes for medium/well-done). Once cooked, leave to rest for 15 minutes (please note that the meat will continue to cook when removed from the heat).

Make the dressing by mixing all the ingredients in a bowl, leave to stand and infuse.

Clean the mushrooms, remove the stalks from the shiitakes, then slice.

Heat the coconut oil in a frying pan, add the sliced shiitake and oyster mushrooms, cook for 5-10 minutes until the juices have evaporated, then add the tamari soy sauce and honey (or preferred choice) and cook for further 3 minutes.

Remove the frying pan from the heat and leave the mushrooms to cool.

Slice the meat as thinly as possible, or to your liking, then add the meat to the mushrooms in the pan to soak up the juices (if you are unsure about the rareness of your meat, you can cook the meat for a couple of minutes on each side with the mushrooms), or just baste all the ingredients together and leave in the pan off the heat.

Wash and finely shred the lettuce, cut the tomatoes in half, and place in a large serving bowl or platter with the cucumber strips.

Place the mushrooms and steak in a separate bowl, then pour over the dressing, stir the mixture a couple of times to ensure that the meat is coated.

Spoon the steak mixture in the centre of your serving dish and sprinkle over the sesame seeds, roughly chopped peanuts and top with coriander.

LISA'S TIP

Exceptionally moreish, you may wish to add a spoon of brown rice or two to help soak up all the wonderful juices!

Thai Chicken Curry

A creamy, citrusy dish full of the
flavours of Southeast Asia.

{serves 4 - 6}

Ingredients

4 chicken breasts (breasts or
thighs), cut into bite-size pieces

2 sweet potatoes, cut into 5cm
strips and then halved

4 tbsp garden peas

400g broccoli florets

1 aubergine, chopped into small
cubes

100g baby corn, cut in half
lengthways

1 tbsp coconut oil (virgin or
odourless)

1 garlic clove, chopped

1-2 tbsp Thai green curry paste
(plus a little extra if you like it
spicy)

1 tbsp Thai fish sauce (Nam pla)

4 tsp palm sugar

3 wide strips lime zest, plus extra to
garnish or lime leaves

1 tsp Madras curry powder
(optional)

2 x 400ml organic coconut milk
(canned)

2 tbsp coconut yogurt

garnish

Thai basil leaves or fresh coriander

wholegrain rice, to serve

Preparation time - 30 mins, cooking Time 20 to 30 mins

Put the sweet potatoes in a pan of boiling water and cook for 5 minutes, then remove with a slotted spoon and throw in the broccoli florets and cook for a further 3 minutes. Remove the broccoli add the baby corn and cook for 3 minutes, by which time all should be just tender. Put to one side.

In a wok or large frying pan, gently heat the oil, add garlic and cook until golden, this should take only a few seconds. Don't let it overcook.

Spoon in the curry paste and stir it around for a few seconds to begin to cook the spices and release all the flavours.

Next, pour in the cream from tin of coconut milk and let it start to bubble. Now add the rest of the tin. Only use one tin at this point.

Stir in the fish sauce and palm sugar. Then add the pieces of chicken, aubergine, cook on a medium to high heat, then turn the heat down to a simmer and cook, covered, for about 15-20 minutes until the chicken is cooked through and the sauce is slightly reduced and thickened.

Tip in the sweet potatoes, broccoli florets, baby corn and garden peas and let them warm through in the sauce, if the coconut milk has reduced too much, add the second tin slowly to 'top up' depending on the amount that you need and cook for a further 10 minutes.

Check for taste as you may wish to add more Thai curry paste at this point.

Then add a lovely 'citrusy' flavour by stirring in the shredded lime leaves (or lime zest). The basil leaves go in next, but only leave them briefly on the heat or they will quickly lose their brightness. Check for seasoning, adding more fish sauce if needed.

Add in 2 tbsp of coconut yogurt and Madras curry powder (optional).

The curry is now best left to sit for a few minutes so the sauce becomes creamier.

Serve with wholegrain rice.

LISA'S TIP

If you have left over roast chicken you can also add towards the end (instead of cooking from raw) to heat through. This recipe will keep for a few days in the refrigerator.

Whole Baked Sea bass in Banana Leaves

The banana leaves make for a bit of 'high drama' at the dinner table. You can also use foil but double it to ensure there are no holes for steam to escape.

{serves 4 - 6}

Ingredients

1 whole sea bass, 1.5kg, scaled, gutted, and fins removed

1 tbsp lime juice mixed

1 tsp sea salt

2 tsp palm sugar

1 tbsp peanut oil

1 tsp sesame oil

cooking string

paste

1 small onion, roughly chopped

1 inch fresh root ginger, peeled and roughly chopped

1 Thai red chilli, deseeded and roughly chopped

2 garlic cloves

1 lemon grass stalk

125ml organic coconut milk (canned)

½ tsp chilli flakes

15g fresh coriander

1-2 tbsp honey, agave nectar or maple syrup

2 large pinches sea salt

banana leaves or foil for wrapping (if using banana leaves, make sure you clean them with warm water and kitchen paper first)

garnish

coriander

lime wedges

Preparation time - 30 mins, cooking time - 30 to 35 mins

Preheat the oven to 400°F gas mark 6, 200°C (180°C fan-assisted).

Wash the sea bass inside and out, pat dry with kitchen paper.

If you are using banana leaves, wash carefully under cold water, and wipe clean with paper towels.

Mix together the lime juice, palm sugar and sea salt and score through the skin of the fish 3-4 times on each side and rub the slits with the lime juice mixture.

Then lay the fish on a large piece of oiled foil or banana leaves using peanut and sesame oil.

Put the lemon grass, chilli, chilli flakes, onion, garlic cloves, coriander, ginger and sea salt into a pestle & mortar or food processor and purée until smooth. Towards the end of grinding or puréeing slowly add 1 - 2 tbsp of honey and the coconut milk.

Season the fish inside and out with the paste, making sure you push some into the scored slits.

To wrap the fish in the banana leaves, begin by folding the sides of the leaf inward, then fold the top and bottom over and tucking the ends under (kind of like making a banana leaf burrito!). Using foil, wrap 2 layers securely around the fish, making sure there are no holes in the parcel. Tie with dampened string if you are using banana leaves.

Place in the pre-heated oven and cook for 30-35 minutes, until flesh is tender, if you're eating the fish straight away, let it rest for about 5 minutes before opening the parcel.

When ready to serve garnish with lime wedges and coriander.

LISA'S TIP

You'll love this tender and wonderful-tasting Thai baked fish. Wrapping the sea bass in a banana leaf ensures the fish remains moist and imparts a subtle flavour. Banana leaves can be found in Thai and certain Asian grocers. However, foil can be used as a substitute. I like to serve with some brown rice to soak up the juices and wok fried pak choi. If you have extra paste, combine it with any leftover coconut milk, heat though in a small saucepan and strain through a fine seive to serve drizzled over the fish as a delicious Thai infused sauce.

Oven Baked Corn Flake Chicken Breast with Salsa

Gluten-free corn flakes make a wonderful substitute for breadcrumbs, and since it is oven-baked rather than fried, you save on calories, too.

··

{serves 4}

Ingredients

4 chicken breasts, skinless 150-200g
gluten-free corn flakes 2 tbsp sesame seeds, toasted
1 egg, beaten
2 tsp honey Dijon mustard
2 tsp Worcestershire sauce, gluten-free or teriyaki sauce
garlic granules
sea salt and white pepper

avocado salsa

1 mango
3 avocados
2 tbsp olive oil
¼ red onion, finely chopped
2 tsp sweet chilli sauce
sea salt and cracked black pepper

garnish

2 limes, cut into wedges
4 handfuls rocket

Preparation time - 40 mins, cooking time - 35 to 40 mins

Preheat the oven to 400°F, gas mark 6, 200°C (180°C fan-assisted).

Line a baking tray with a silicone baking mat or parchment paper.

Wash your chicken breasts and dry with paper towels.

Place the corn flakes in a plastic bag and crush with your hands until the flakes have broken down. On a plate, combine with a sprinkle of sesame seeds, sea salt and white pepper and toss together.

In a separate bowl large enough to hold two chicken breasts at a time, crack the whole egg and beat.

Season the egg with the Worcestershire sauce or teriyaki sauce, honey Dijon mustard, garlic granules and a bit more sea salt and white pepper.

Coat the chicken breast in the egg mixture then carefully place the chicken breast on the plate with the seasoned corn flakes, and coat both sides, repeat with the remaining breasts, place on the baking tray.

Cook in the pre-heated oven for 35-40 minutes, ensuring presentation side (rounded part of the breast) is facing up.

To make the avocado salsa, halve the avocados, remove the stone and peel away the skin, cut the flesh into 1cm cubes, and place in a large bowl.

Peel the mango and cut both sides close to the pip, then into 1cm cubes, then add to the same bowl as the avocado, mix together with the finely chopped red onion.

Add the olive oil, sweet chili and season with sea salt and black pepper.

Gently stir the ingredients, you can mash the avocado slightly, but keep it quite chunky.

Remove the chicken breasts from the oven and rest for 8 minutes before cutting.

Garnish with the avocado salsa with rocket and a wedge or two of lime.

LISA'S TIP

The mango has an oblong pit in the centre. Cut along the sides of the pit, separating the flesh from the pit then taking a mango half, use a knife to make lengthwise and crosswise cuts in it, but try not to cut through the peel. At this point you may be able to peel the segments right off of the peel with your fingers.

Frozen Berries Coconut Sorbet

A delicious dairy free treat that doesn't require an ice cream maker. You can eat this as soon as it's made if you like a soft scoop – or freeze overnight for a firmer texture.

....

{serves 4}

Ingredients

2 bananas ripe, frozen (3cm slices)

125g blackberries, frozen

300g strawberries, stems removed, frozen

200g blueberries, frozen

100g coconut milk yogurt (coyo)

2 tsp date or maple syrup

2 handfuls of granola, gluten-free

Preparation time - 20 mins, freezing fruit 6 to 8 hours (overnight - is best) freezing sorbet 6 to 8 hours (overnight- is best)

Remove the frozen fruits from the freezer 20 minutes before blending.

Place all the frozen fruits in the bowl of your food processor and process for 1 minute at a time, stirring with a spatula as required. Repeat 3-4 times until well blended.

Add the coconut yogurt together with the date or maple syrup and blend for another 30 seconds.

Transfer to a freezer safe container and freeze until required or serve immediately.

When serving, sprinkle some granola over the top.

LISA'S TIP
A good first dessert to make with children. A sneaky way to get in your five-a-day!

Seasonal Fruit Tart with Crème Patisserie

Admittedly, this recipe takes time but be patient. The result is a stunning dessert which resembles a painter's palette of brilliant colours.

{serves 10-12}

date & walnut pastry

300 pitted dates
250g ground walnuts
150g ground almonds
pinch sea salt

Crème Patisserie

600ml almond milk
1 vanilla pod, deseeded
6 egg yolks (large)
100g coconut sugar
50g oat flour, gluten-free
10g cornflour

Seasonal Fruit

500g strawberries, hulled and thinly sliced
150g blueberries
1 tbsp apricot jam (sugar free, smooth variety)
1 tsp cold water

Preparation time - 2 hours, cooling - 30 to 40 mins

To make the pastry you will need a food processor.

Place the dates in the food processor, and blend until smooth then add the ground walnuts and almonds, a pinch of sea salt and process until smooth.

When the pastry forms into a ball, stop the machine.

Line the base of a 23cm fluted, loose bottom non-stick tart tin with parchment paper. Then, by hand, push the mixture into the base and against the sides to form the pastry for the tart, ensuring it is level all the way around and on the base.

Place another piece of parchment paper over the pasty and place in the freezer for 20 minutes. Remove and place in the fridge.

To make the crème patisserie, cut the vanilla pod in half lengthways. Remove the seeds with the back of a knife running down the length of the pod. Place the seeds and pod into the almond milk in a saucepan on a gentle heat for 5 minutes for the vanilla to infuse the milk (be careful that the milk does not burn).

Place the egg yolks and sugar together in a bowl and beat until smooth. Now slowly whisk in the oat flour and cornflour until you have a smooth paste.

Remove the milk from the stove, then slowly whisk the milk into the egg mixture using a balloon whisk. Mix slowly and carefully until all the ingredients are thoroughly blended.

Pour the liquid through a sieve directly into the saucepan, pushing through the vanilla seeds. Discard the pod.

Place back on the stove and bring the vanilla cream to the boil, whisking it continuously. Continue to cook for 2-3 minutes to get rid of the starchy taste of the corn flour. It is important to continue whisking or the mixture will stick.

LISA'S TIP

To decorate the tart its best to use fresh fruits (such as berries, bananas, oranges, kiwifruit, plums, pineapple, and melon). Prepare the fruit by gently washing and drying. Peel and slice the bananas, plums and kiwifruit. The strawberries will need to be sliced also. Arranging the fruit on the tart can be done either randomly or in concentric overlapping circles, starting at the outside edge. Try to cover the filling completely so none of the cream mixture shows.

If you feel that you haven't reached the correct consistency after 3 minutes, reduce the heat to medium/low and continue whisking. You should start to feel the crème thickening and you will notice your hand aching by now, but don't give up! You are looking for a thick consistency (once again be careful not to burn the cream).

Pour the vanilla cream into a bowl or baking tray to cool, cover with cling film and place in the fridge for 30-40 minutes until chilled.

Remove the pastry from the fridge.

Prepare all your fruits by washing and slicing, so that everything is ready to hand.

Remove the crème patisserie from the fridge, beat the mixture together until smooth, if necessary the thick cold cream can be strained through a fine sieve and stirred until smooth, then place the mixture into a piping bag.

Pipe out the crème patisserie starting in the middle and follow around in a circle motion until you get to the edge then smooth out with the back of a spoon

Assemble your mixed fruit of strawberries and blueberries.

For the apricot glaze: heat the apricot jam in a small saucepan over a medium heat until it has melted. You can add a touch of water if the consistency is too thick, let cool until it is only slightly warm, then using a pastry brush glaze the tart.

Banana Ice Cream with Halva

This is my favourite magic trick in the kitchen: creamy ice cream made with just bananas! The other ingredients are added just for fun. Now gather around and watch!

....

{serves 4 - 6}

Ingredients

6 ripe bananas, cut into 3cm slices, frozen
100g vanilla halva, chopped
40g dark chocolate, melted
40g banana chips, chopped

Preparation time - 20 mins, freezing time - 4 to 6 hours (or overnight is best)

Peel the bananas and cut into 3cm slices and place in a freezer bag or zip lock containers and freeze until solid - around 4 to 6 hours, or overnight is best.

Place the banana chips in a food processor and process until fully chopped.

Melt the dark chocolate and leave to cool slightly.

Remove the bananas 5-10 minutes before processing to help thaw out.

Place the bananas in the food processor and blend away, you will have to keep scraping down the sides every so often.

Watch as the magic happens when bananas turn into ice-cream! It should take approx. 3 minutes. At first you will think 'how is this ever going to be soft and creamy?' The answer is *patience* and wait for the surprise!

Within a few minutes, you'll be able to process the mixture into a thick and creamy, ice-cream-like dessert.

Scoop out into a large bowl add fold in the chopped halva.

Serve with melted chocolate and sprinkled with chopped banana chips.

Then serve straight away to your guests if you like it semi-soft. Or you can freeze for a few hours to make it scoop-able.

LISA'S TIP

Freeze ripe bananas until solid, then whiz them up in a blender or food processor, it gets creamy and a little gooey, just like ice cream. And what's more exciting it has no additional dairy, wheat, gluten, sweeteners, additives or preservatives! For toppings try: crushed almonds and honey, cocoa powder and cashew butter, granola, or even some more sliced bananas.

Raw Blueberry Cheesecake

Made with a vegan crust, this dairy free cheesecake is surprisingly delicious – bursting with antioxidants from the blueberries.

{serves 4 - 6}

crust ingredients

100g macadamia nuts

150g blanched almonds

50g desiccated coconut

200g dates, pre-soak if hard

3 tsp lemon juice

1 pinch sea salt

cheesecake layer ingredients

350g cashews, soaked overnight in water, then rinsed and drained on paper towel until ready to use

60ml coconut oil (virgin or odourless)

60ml honey, agave nectar or maple syrup

2 tsp custard powder

5 tsp lemon juice

100g blueberries (splitting the mixture)

blueberry chia seed topping

240g blueberries

4 tsp honey, agave nectar or maple syrup

6 tsp chia seeds

2 tsp lemon juice

Preparation time - 60 mins, soaking time - 8 hours (or overnight is best)

First, pre-soak the cashews, cover with cold water, overnight or for 8 hours.

Line the base and sides of 20cm non-stick springform tin with parchment paper.

To make the chia seed topping, place the blueberries in the food processor and blend until smooth. Sieve over a bowl to omit the skins and seeds. Add agave nectar (or preferred choice), lemon juice, and chia seeds. Mix together then refrigerate for 2 hours.

For the crust, place the macadamia, blanched almonds and coconut into your food processor and pulse until a chunky sandy consistency. Place into a clean bowl.

Add the dates, lemon and salt to the food processor, blend until smooth and then add the macadamia nut mixture back into the food processor, and blend until it forms a ball.

Place the nut and date mixture into your prepared tin, press down firmly and place in the freezer.

Place all cheesecake filling ingredients (expect blueberries) into your food processor and blend for 5 minutes until completely smooth (stopping to scrape down the sides).

Remove the crust after 10 minutes from the freezer.

Pour about 1/2 of the filling mixture onto the crust and smooth with a spatula, then place back in the freezer.

Add the blueberries to the remaining filling and blend on high until smooth, then pour onto the first layer of filling. Place in freezer until solid - about 2 hours.

Then add the chia seed topping. The seeds will have started to congeal together so loosen them slightly, then smooth over the cheesecake and decorate with blueberries and place back in the fridge to set for 1 hour.

Release the cake from the tin when ready to serve.

LISA'S TIP

Cheesecakes are always a good place to start when making raw desserts because the process is so quick and simple. And what's more exciting is that it's wheat, gluten and dairy free.

AUTUMN

seasonal moods

Without warning the days gain a crisp, energising feel and the trees put on their autumn coats. Burnt oranges, vibrant reds and golden brown is the palette of autumn both in the landscape and on our plates.

Apples, pumpkins, and sweet potatoes are in abundance and combined with a touch of ginger, turn magical. The smell of roasting chestnuts or the simply oven-seared figs add to the fragrance of Autumn.

It is the time of year when we take stock and review where we've been. Is it a path to continue or to change?

APPLES Crisp English apples perfectly sum up the arrival of autumn. Containing bone strengthening boron and cholesterol lowering pectin, the old expression might be right! Try apple cider vinegar on salads for additional benefits.

FIGS Look for slightly soft and ripe figs when shopping as they don't ripen once picked. Naturally sweet, figs are ideal for healthier baking. Also, its potassium content is high which serves to negate the effects of sodium on the body.

CHESTNUTS The warm, nutty smell of roasting chestnuts is one of the joys of this season. They are also low in fat, high in fibre and chock full of minerals. Eat them to help boost your immune system.

GINGER Ginger has been prescribed for hundreds of years to relieve digestive problems, but new research shows that this root's real power is in reducing inflammation. Look for a thin skin variety when shopping as this indicates the ginger is young.

BUTTERNUT SQUASH Offers a great source of vitamins B1, B6 and C. Perfect now as vitamin C boosts your immune system. Like beets, try butternut squash roasted for exceptional flavour!

PEARS Often described as hypoallergenic (allergies to them are rare), pears are often the first fruit we taste. They are considered the perfect weaning food for babies who are attempting solids. As adults, we love them poached in red wine or served with melted dark chocolate.

AUBERGINES Whether you called them 'aubergine', 'eggplant' or 'brinjal', this vegetable – which is actually a berry – can be found all over the world in local cuisine. Originally grown in India they can now be found in many shapes, sizes and colours around the globe.

PECANS The buttery and almost maple-syrup like tang of pecan nuts is unmistakable. Part of the hickory family, pecans originate from the Americas and are among the top 15 most anti-oxidant-rich foods.

Dried Fig, Pecan & Dark Chocolate Oat Bars

Slightly decadent, but less so than store-bought brands, these
bars are good for breakfast or as a lunch box treat.

....

{makes 16 bars}

ingredients

150ml coconut oil (virgin or
odourless)

120g honey, agave nectar or
maple syrup

2 tbsp date syrup

225g rolled oats, gluten-free

20g sunflower seeds

60g pecans, chopped in half

100g dried figs, sliced into strips

35g dark chocolate raisins

20g desiccated coconut

2 pinches sea salt

1 tsp cinnamon

Preparation time - 30 mins, cooking time - 35 to 40 mins, refrigeration
time - 1 hour to firm

Preheat the oven to 300°F gas mark 2, 150°C (130°C fan-assisted).

Line a 23cm x 23cm baking tray with parchment paper.

Over a gentle heat, melt the coconut oil, agave nectar (or preferred
choice) and date syrup until smooth and set aside.

In a large mixing bowl add the rolled oats, salt, cinnamon, chopped
pecans, sliced dried figs, desiccated coconut, sunflower seeds and
dark chocolate raisins. Mix well.

Pour over the oil mixture, mix well and then place in the prepared
baking tray. Press down firmly until smooth.

Bake in the preheated oven for 35-40 minutes or until golden.

Let cool in the baking tray, then place in the fridge to harden up.

When ready to serve, lift out of the tin and cut into squares. Place
back in the fridge if you have spare.

Yum.

LISA'S TIP

*These oat bars can be stored in an airtight container for up to one
week in the refrigerator. These are perfect for breakfast on the run as
they are filled with protein and fibre. Once you start to perfect these
bars, you can play around with the nut and fruit ingredients.*

Shakshuka

This is my version and it has a twist! I'm not a fan of peppers, so I add shiitake mushrooms and kale. If you want more heat, add some chilli flakes or a touch of Tabasco.

{serves 4 -6}

ingredients

6 large eggs
500ml pasta tomato sauce (jarred)
50g curly kale, stems removed
1 large onion, thinly sliced
125g shiitake mushrooms, thinly sliced, stems removed
4 tbsp rapeseed oil
sea salt and white pepper
garlic granules

garnish

cracked black pepper

Preparation time - 30 mins, cooking time - 31 to 33 mins

Heat the rapeseed oil in a large frying pan and sauté the thinly sliced onions for 5 minutes until soft and translucent.

Add the sliced shiitake mushrooms, cook for 2 minutes and at this point you should notice the mushrooms soaking up the oil. Season well with sea salt, white pepper and garlic granules and cook for further 3 minutes.

Add the curly kale and cook for 5 minutes, continuously stirring.

Pour in the tomato sauce and cook for 10 minutes on a low light to reduce the sauce.

Remove from the heat, crack the egg into a wine glass, then make a little well in the sauce and pour in the whole egg, repeat with each egg.

Place the frying pan back on the heat and cook covered for 6-8 minutes until the egg is set.

Then serve straight from the pan with a sprinkle of black pepper.

LISA'S TIP

"What the heck is Shakshuka?" you might be asking. It's a delicious tomatoey (sometimes spicy) Middle Eastern egg dish that's become very popular. I love to serve this dish with fresh avocado on the side and some gluten-free bread to wipe up the delicious sauce!

Bircher Autumnal Muesli

Usually had at breakfast, this dish also
makes a scrumptious dessert!

....

{serves 4 - 6}

ingredients

200g jumbo rolled oats, gluten-free

10g pistachios whole

10g almonds whole

10g pecans, whole

20g sultanas

4 dried figs, cut into small strips
(remove stalk)

1 pinky lady apple, cored and
grated (keep skin on)

2 tbsp honey, agave nectar or
maple syrup

600ml almond milk

2 tbsp coconut yogurt (coyo)

cinnamon, sprinkle

garnish

2 figs quartered

1 tbsp honey, agave nectar or
maple syrup

2 pinches coconut sugar

handful desiccated coconut

Preparation time - 20 mins, refrigeration 8 hours (overnight)

In a large mixing bowl, add the rolled oats, cinnamon, grated apple, pistachios, almonds, pecans, sultanas and dried figs. Mix well.

In a measuring jug, add the almond milk, agave nectar, and coconut yogurt. Beat together with a mini hand whisk or fork, then pour over the oats.

Gently stir everything together, then cover and place in the fridge for 8 hours.

Preheat the oven to 350°F, gas mark 4, 180°C (160°C fan-assisted).

Line a small baking tray with a silicone baking mat or parchment paper, place the quartered figs on the tray, drizzle with honey (or preferred choice) and 2 pinches of coconut sugar.

Bake in the preheated oven for 10 minutes, then leave to cool.

When ready to serve, put the bircher muesli in serving bowls, place the quartered figs on top and drizzle a little juice from the figs and sprinkle with desiccated coconut.

LISA'S TIP

I love to have a big batch of bircher muesli in the fridge, it's the perfect breakfast when you're in a hurry. You can keep this in the fridge for 2-3 days. Be adventurous with your fillings, once you get the hang of making it. For cooler mornings heat the Bircher muesli on the stove for 2-3 minutes.

Sweet Potato Latke with Poached Eggs

While this is a complete dish, consider using the latkes alone to be served with a hearty beef stew. For something a bit special, add quail's eggs instead.

{makes 10 Latkes}

ingredients

675g Maris Piper potatoes (approx. 3 large), grated

250g sweet potato, grated

1 white onion, grated

60g fine cornmeal flour, sifted

½ tsp baking powder, gluten-free

1 large egg

1 large egg yolk

500ml rapeseed oil

sea salt and white pepper

garnish

4 tbsp crème fraîche

225g smoked salmon

4 large eggs

2 tsp vinegar

small handful chives, chopped

sprigs of dill

Preparation time - 60 mins, cooking time - 20 mins

Grate the potatoes using the coarse side of the grater or a food processor. Place in a clean tea towel and squeeze out as much liquid as you can, then place the potato in a bowl (you want your moisture from other ingredients, not the potato).

Grate the sweet potato and onion and place in the same bowl as the white potato. In a separate bowl, beat the whole egg, and egg yolk. Season generously with sea salt and white pepper and mix well with potato mixture.

Add the sifted fine cornmeal flour and mix well. Using a 2.5cm round cutter, place a large tablespoon of filling into the cutter, with a chopping board underneath, squeeze the filling until level, lift off the cutter and repeat with the remaining mixture.

Place a large frying pan on the stove, add the oil on a medium/high heat. Using a spatula carefully slide off the latkes into the hot oil, fry over moderate heat until brown on the underside (approx. 3-4 minutes), then flip over using a fork and spatula (approx. 3-4 minutes) until crisp and golden.

Remove from the pan, drain on paper towel and serve hot. Keep a lined tray ready for the latkes to keep warm in the oven as you make more batches… They'll also cook through a little more in the oven. Don't stack! You can't leave the latkes in the frying pan too long because the natural sugar content of the sweet potato will blacken easily - which is why it's important you don't have your stovetop heat on too high.

Bring water and 2 tsp vinegar to the boil then lower to a simmer and poach the eggs to your liking for 3-4 minutes, take out with a slotted spoon and dry on paper towels.

Stack two potato pancakes per person with the egg on top. Add a spoonful of crème fraîche, with a sprig of dill and a smoked salmon flower (roll the smoked salmon and crunch together by the sides), and sprinkle over the chives.

LISA'S TIP

Always use fresh eggs when poaching and add a little vinegar to the water. This holds the egg's protein together. Another trick is to break the eggs into a cup first, then add to the simmering water.

Cauliflower Pizza Base with Blue Cheese, Pear & Walnuts

I can sense you are scratching your head at this one
– trust me, it works and is absolutely delicious!

....

{makes an 8 - 10inch pizza}

ingredients

1 medium cauliflower head
70g grated mozzarella cheese (50g for the crust/20g for the topping)
1 egg, beaten
garlic granules
sea salt and white pepper

topping

1 pear, thinly sliced
20g walnuts
50g blue cheese, crumbled
olive oil, mild
sea salt and cracked black pepper

garnish

rocket leaves
sea salt and pepper to taste
cracked black pepper

Preparation time - 60 mins, cooking time - 28 to 30 mins

Preheat the oven to 400°F, gas mark 6, 200°C (180°C fan-assisted) and pre-line a baking tray with a silicone baking mat or parchment paper.

Wash and thoroughly dry the cauliflower. Cut off the florets, you don't need much stem, just stick with the florets. Pulse in your food processor for about 30 seconds, until you get powdery snow-like cauliflower. Place the cauliflower in a microwave safe bowl and cover, microwave for 4 minutes or steam. When cooked, place onto a clean tea towel and allow to cool.

Now wrap up the cauliflower in the tea towel and wring out all the liquid. Don't be alarmed with what you have left! Place the cauliflower into a bowl and add 50g of the grated mozzarella cheese. Beat the egg, season generously with sea salt, white pepper and garlic granules. Pour onto the cauliflower mixture and combine well. Now use your hands to form the 'dough' into a crust on your parchment paper (aim for about 8-10 inches/20cm-25cm). Pat it down thoroughly, you want it nice and tightly formed together, don't make it too thick or thin either.

Bake for 20 minutes, until it starts to turn golden brown. Remove from the oven. Leave the base to cool for 5-10 minutes, then carefully turn over the base and place back on the tray. Drizzle a little olive oil and season with sea salt, black pepper on the cauliflower base, then top with thinly sliced pear, scatter with blue cheese and walnuts.

Season with a little sea salt and black pepper and olive oil. Top with the remaining grated mozzarella cheese and bake in the oven for 8-10 minutes. Garnish with rocket, olive oil and season lightly with black pepper and sea salt.

LISA'S TIP

This is the best invention ever! Especially if you are following a gluten-free diet. Add whatever toppings you like! Who would have thought you could make a pizza base out of a vegetable! It's so delicious, that you won't think twice about wishing you made it with flour and yeast! And yes you can pick it up just like a real pizza!

Aromatic Crispy Duck Salad

One of the most popular dishes I make,
I often make two ducks at a time!

{serves 4 - 6}

ingredients

1 whole duck, roughly 2kg in weight

Chinese 5 spice powder

pinch of sea salt

1 onion

7 tbsp hoisin sauce, gluten-free, plus a bit extra

garnish

1 ½ tbsp sesame oil

1 large cucumber, deseeded (julienned or spiralised)

crispy salad onions (gluten-free)

sesame seeds, toasted

2 handfuls cashew nuts, toasted

Preparation time - 40 mins, cooking time - 1 hour 52 mins

Preheat the oven to 400°F, gas mark 6, 200°C (180°C fan-assisted).

Wash and thoroughly dry the duck with a paper towel. Drying it makes the skin crispy. Using a wooden skewer, prick the upper part of the breast and in-between the breast and thigh. Cut the onion into quarters, keeping the root intact. Rub 1 tbsp of sesame oil over both sides of the duck. Season with salt and Chinese 5 spice inside and out of the cavity.

Place the duck on a wire rack over a large foil-lined baking tray. Bake in the preheated oven for 1 hour, breast facing down. Remove from the oven and carefully turn, breast facing up. Bake for 20 minutes then turn over, breast down. Reduce temperature to 300°F, gas mark 2, 150°C (130°C fan-assisted) for 20 minutes. Remove, leaving the duck to rest for 10 minutes.

Take off all the skin and place it on a clean, foil-lined tray. Rub in 1 tbsp hoisin sauce then increase the oven temperature back to 400°F, gas mark 6, 200°C (180°C fan-assisted) and bake for 10-12 minutes until crispy. Remove the duck bones and shred the meat into a large mixing bowl. When slightly cooled, add 3 tbsp hoisin sauce and massage into the meat. Let cool completely.

Deseed the cucumber then julienne or spiralise it.

On a large serving platter place the cucumber, drizzle with 2 tsp sesame oil, then sprinkle with toasted sesame seeds. Add the shredded duck and top with shredded crispy skin. To garnish, drizzle 2-3 tbsp hoisin sauce and sprinkle a few toasted sesame seeds, crispy salad onions and toasted cashew nuts on top.

LISA'S TIP

Both children and adults go mad for this salad! Serve with Chinese style pancakes on the side should you wish! I like to use baby gem lettuce instead.

Fresh Fig & Goats Cheese Salad

A simple and yet delectable salad of grilled fruit and nuts all served with a walnut oil and honey fig dressing. Makes for an elegant lunch or a refreshing starter.

....

{serves 4 - 6}

ingredients

8 fresh figs, 4 cut in half and 4 make a cut like a cross in the top of each fig

150g goats cheese, crumbled

2 tsp honey, agave nectar or maple syrup

2 handfuls walnuts, crumbled

1 handful pistachios, roughly chopped

2 handfuls pomegranate seeds

1 large handful rocket

2 tbsp walnut oil

sea salt and cracked black pepper

Preparation time - 30 mins, cooking time - 10 mins

Preheat the grill to a high setting, line a baking tray with foil or parchment paper.

Wash and stem the figs.

Slice 4 figs in half and arrange cut side up in a baking dish together. With the remaining 4 figs, cut a cross in the top of the figs to about half way down the fig so that they open up a bit if gently squeezed at the bottom.

Drizzle the honey (or preferred choice) over the top of the figs.

Roast for about 10 minutes, or until the honey (or preferred choice) is just beginning to bubble.

The figs should not be too soft, be careful not to burn them - you need to be able to pick them up with your fingers.

Let cool for about 10 minutes before assembling the salad (keep the juice from the tray).

Place the figs on the serving platter. Scatter over the crumbled goats cheese, crumbled walnuts, roughly chopped pistachios and pomegranate seeds.

Drizzle with walnut or olive oil and 1 tbsp of fig juice from the baking tray.

Sprinkle a little sea salt and black pepper then garnish with rocket.

Savour.

LISA'S TIP

This recipe could be varied by using different honey choices. Try orange blossom, or flavour-infused honeys like lavender, rosemary, lemon or cinnamon. You can also drizzle over some balsamic glaze if you'd prefer.

Honey & Soy Baked Salmon

Ideal for introducing fish to the pickiest of eaters. If you like a bit of a kick, add a bit of lime juice and chilli flakes to the marinade.

....

{serves 4}

ingredients

4 salmon fillets, skin on

5 tbsp orange juice

5 tbsp honey, agave nectar or maple syrup

4½ tbsp. tamari soy sauce, gluten-free

1 tbsp minced fresh ginger

5 garlic cloves, minced

1 tsp rapeseed oil

1 tsp sesame oil

salt and black pepper

garnish

250g buckwheat soba gluten-free noodles

sesame seeds

Preparation time - 30 mins, cooking time - 12 to 15 mins (20 mins well cooked)

Preheat the oven to 375°F, gas mark 5, 190°C (170°C fan-assisted).

In a non-stick small saucepan, pour in orange juice, honey (or preferred choice), tamari soy sauce, garlic and ginger. Heat gently over a medium heat, stirring only once for approximately one minute, then remove and leave to cool completely. Now pass through a sieve and discard the garlic and ginger. In a large non-stick frying pan, heat the oils over a gentle heat. Remove from the heat, place the salmon fillets in the pan, flesh side down, for 30 seconds. Flip over using kitchen tongs and place back on a medium heat to get the skin crispy (approx. 1-2 minutes) then remove from the heat and cool completely.

Season the flesh side with a touch of salt and black pepper. If you have time, marinate the salmon. When the fish is cold, place in a large freezer bag with half of the cooled marinade and chill for at least 30 minutes or overnight, turning the bag a couple of times. Line a baking tray with parchment paper or foil. Place the salmon fillets on the tray and if you haven't marinated the fish, pour ½ of your marinade over the salmon fillets, keeping the remaining marinade in the non-stick saucepan.

Bake in the preheated oven for 15-20 minutes. Reduce to 12 minutes if you like your salmon slightly rare in the middle. Bring the reserved marinade to a light boil in the small saucepan over a medium heat, cook for 5 minutes or until slightly thickened and syrupy.

Cook the buckwheat soba noodles as directed on the packaging. When the salmon is cooked, remove from the oven tray and pour over the remaining marinade. Sprinkle with sesame seeds and serve with buckwheat soba gluten-free noodles.

LISA'S TIP

To avoid overcooking, remain close to your oven. Remove fish promptly when your timer goes off. If it looks almost or just barely done (just barely pink all the way through), you've timed things perfectly, as it will finish cooking outside the oven.

Roasted Aubergine with Tahini & Pomegranate

A beautiful dish which marries jewel-like pomegranate
seeds with the black skin of the aubergines.

....

{serves 4 - 6}

ingredients

3 large aubergines
½ pomegranate, deseeded
4 tbsp extra virgin olive oil
2 tsp sesame oil
sea salt and cracked black pepper
garlic granules

tahini dressing

3 tbsp tahini paste
4 tbsp cold water
squeeze of lemon
1 garlic clove, minced
sea salt

garnish

pomegranate seeds
2 tbsp sesames seeds, toasted
2 tbsp honey, agave nectar or
maple syrup
1 handful fresh coriander

Preparation time - 40 mins, cooking time - 50 to 60 mins

Preheat the oven to 350°F, gas mark 4, 180°C (160°C fan-assisted).

Wash and pat dry the aubergines, then cut in half lengthwise (keeping the stalk on).

With the tip of a knife, score the flesh deeply in a diamond criss-cross pattern by making five or six long cuts on the diagonal, cutting at a steep angle and then rotating the aubergine to make another set of similar cuts (do not cut through to the skin).

Brush both sides with the 2 tbsp. extra virgin olive oil and sesame oil.

Put the aubergines cut-side facing up on a baking tray lined with silicone baking mat or parchment paper.

Season with sea salt, black pepper and garlic granules, place in the preheated oven and bake for 40-50 minutes.

Place in the preheated oven and bake for 40 minutes, then remove from the oven and turn the aubergines over and bake for another 10 minutes facing upwards.

Check often to make sure that they do not burn. If your aubergines still aren't tender all the way through, bake for a further 5-10 minutes, then proceed with the rest of the recipe.

Remove from the oven, drizzle with 2 tbsp extra virgin olive oil, then leave to cool.

To make the tahini dressing, add the tahini paste, water, lemon, minced garlic clove and season with sea salt then mix either by hand or in mini food processor.

Place the roasted aubergines around a large platter, spooning the tahini paste around and over the aubergines.

Drizzle acacia honey around the plate and over the aubergines.

Then garnish with the toasted sesame seeds, fresh coriander and pomegranate seeds.

LISA'S TIP

Aubergines have a wonderfully 'meaty' texture and can be roasted in their skins until charred, so the pulp can be removed and blended with other ingredients, such as lemon, tahini, and garlic, as in the Middle Eastern dish baba ghanoush or the similar Greek dish, melitzanosaltata.

Butternut Squash & Carrot Soup

A heavenly shade of orange, the true colour of autumn leaves,
this soup looks fabulous served in a 'squash bowl'.

{serves 8}

ingredients

2 large butternut squash, peeled
and cubed (keep seeds for roasting)
2 large Echalion shallots, sliced
6 carrots, cubed
½ litre vegetable stock, gluten-free
½ litre chicken stock, gluten-free
½ litre boiling water
2 tbsp olive oil
sea salt and white pepper

garnish

chives
roasted butternut squash seeds (see
Lisa's tip for instructions)
coconut yogurt (coyo)

Preparation time - 30 mins, cooking time - 40 mins

In a large saucepan on medium heat, sauté the shallots in olive oil until translucent (approx. 5 minutes).

Add the cubed butternut squash, continue to sauté for 3 minutes then add the cubed carrots.

Season with sea salt and white pepper.

Add your vegetable, chicken stock and boiling water. Increase the heat and bring the soup to boil for 3-5 minutes.

Reduce the heat to medium and cook for 40 minutes (if you find there is a lot of broth on the top, using a large spoon you can skim this off).

Remove from the heat and cool slightly.

Using a hand held blender, purée the soup in the pot, or purée in batches in a blender or food processor.

If the soup is too thick, add a little extra boiling water (almond milk or soya milk are also good choices).

Garnish with coconut yogurt, roasted butternut squash seeds and chives.

LISA'S TIP

To make the squash bowl, cut the butternut squash just beyond the bulbous part of the squash where it meets the neck. Using a spoon, scoop out the seeds. Rinse the seeds to remove fibres and also the inside of the bulbous part of the butternut squash. Pat dry with kitchen towel. Preheat the oven to 350°F, gas mark 4, 180°C (160°C fan-assisted). Line a baking tray with parchment paper, place the butternut squash and seeds on the tray, and drizzle olive oil over. Sprinkle with sea salt and cracked black pepper. Roast the butternut squash uncovered for 40-50 minutes, but remove the seeds after 20-25 minutes. Season with a little touch of salt while the seeds are cooling. The toasted seeds will keep for several months in a sealed container. Serve your soup in the squash and top with the roasted seeds! PS - You can eat the skin of the butternut squash, enjoy!

Sweet Potato Gratin

A healthier version of the classic potato gratin with the refreshing flavours of fresh coriander and coconut milk.

{serves 4}

ingredients

3 large sweet potatoes, peeled and sliced on a mandolin

2 onions, finely sliced

2 tbsp coconut oil (virgin or odourless)

2 garlic cloves, crushed

1 large handful fresh coriander, finely chopped

2 tsp palm or coconut sugar

200ml organic coconut milk (canned)

60g medium cornmeal

sea salt, white pepper and cracked black pepper

chilli flakes

Preparation time - 30 mins, cooking time - 60 mins

Preheat the oven to 375°F, gas mark 5, 190°C (170°C fan-assisted).

In a non-stick frying pan sauté the onions in coconut oil until soft and translucent, then season with sea salt, white pepper and chilli flakes.

Add the crushed garlic cloves, palm sugar and chopped coriander to the onions and continue to cook over a gentle heat, then set aside.

Slice sweet potatoes into thin slices using a mandolin or carefully with a knife.

In a 23cm circular or oval Pyrex dish, lay the sautéed onions around the base.

Cover with the sweet potatoes overlapping in a concertina, season with a little sea salt and black pepper as you layer each level.

Pour the coconut milk over the sweet potatoes, until covered.

In a small bowl season the medium cornmeal with sea salt and white pepper, then sprinkle over the sweet potatoes to cover the dish.

Bake, uncovered, for about 60 minutes, rotating the pan in the oven after 30 minutes to ensure uniform baking.

When the potatoes are tender and the topping is crisp and golden brown, remove from the oven and let sit for 2 to 3 minutes so the potatoes can absorb some extra liquid.

If your topping isn't crispy when about to serve, pop under the grill for 1-2 minutes, keeping an eye on it, so it doesn't burn.

LISA'S TIP

Serve hot or cold with fish, chicken or meat. Sprinkle with toasted chopped pecans for a seasonal garnish. Place chopped nuts in a dry, non-stick pan on medium-high heat. Stirring occasionally, toast the nuts until aromatic, approximately 2-3 minutes being careful not to burn.

Chicken & Sweet Corn Soup

An incredibly silky soup, which once again shows that you don't have to give up your take-away favourites!

....

{serves 4 - 6}

ingredients

1 litre chicken stock, gluten-free

375g canned creamed style corn
(Green Giant brand preferred)

198g canned sweet corn, sieved
(Green Giant brand preferred)

2 tsp tamari soy sauce, gluten-free

3 tsp cornflour

2 tbsp cold water

2 eggs, lightly beaten

150g cooked chicken breast,
shredded (optional)

garnish

spring onion, sliced

tamari soy sauce, gluten-free

Preparation time - 20 mins, cooking time - 10 mins

Heat up the chicken stock in a large saucepan.

Add the creamed corn and sieved sweet corn.

In a small mixing bowl combine the cornflour with 2 tbsp cold water and stir.

Add the tamari soy sauce to the chicken stock, continue stirring for 5 minutes.

Add the cornflour mixture to thicken the soup and the shredded chicken (if using), increase to medium/high heat and cook for a further 5 minutes.

Take off the heat and after 5 minutes, check for seasoning.

Gently beat the eggs in a small bowl and using a fork gently swirl in the lightly beaten egg little by little in the soup through the fork's tines – then stir the soup gently in a circular motion. This should yield delicate egg strips which disperse throughout the soup.

Serve with a garnish of spring onion.

LISA'S TIP

Sweet corn chicken soup is my favourite Chinese soup. It is one of the simplest soup recipes that can be made at home, and I guarantee you that this soup will give any good Chinese restaurant a run for its money!

Parsnips with Sesame & Honey

Small touches, such as toasted seeds, make a bigger
than expected difference to everyday vegetables.

....

{serves 4 - 6}

ingredients

6 parsnips, peeled, cut lengthways
into 4 to 6 strips

2 tbsp olive oil

sea salt and cracked black pepper

paprika

1-2 tbsp honey, agave nectar or
maple syrup

1 handful sesame seeds

Preparation time - 30 mins, cooking time - 40 to 45 mins

Preheat the oven to 375°F, gas mark 5, 190°C (170°C fan-assisted).

Line a baking tray with silicone baking mat or parchment paper.

Toast the sesame seeds: heat a heavy bottom frying pan to hot but
not burning. Add the sesame seeds to the dry, hot pan and gently
swirl the pan around until you notice the seeds starting to colour.
Place on a plate immediately. They will continue to cook even
when off the heat. Set aside.

Peel all the parsnips and cut in half lengthways then each half either
into two or three strips depending on size (ensure all parsnips
spears are of a similar size).

Place the parsnips on your lined baking tray, season generously with
sea salt, black pepper and paprika.

Rub these seasonings into the parsnip then coat in olive oil.

Place in the pre-heated oven for 40 minutes, although keep an eye
on them, turning them over after the first 20 minutes.

After 40 minutes, drizzle the honey (or preferred choice) over the
parsnips and cook for a further 5 minutes.

Remove the parsnips from the oven and place on your serving
platter or plates and sprinkle the toasted sesame seeds over the top.

LISA'S TIP
*You can enjoy these parsnips cold too, chop them up in a salad, or
add them to a frittata.*

Aubergine Sauce with Courgette Spaghetti

Courgette spirals makes a surprisingly tasty alternative to pasta. This aubergine sauce can also be cooked separately and used as a side dish or as a topping for quinoa.

{serves 4 - 6}

ingredients

2 large aubergines, cut into small cubes (approx. 1cm)

2 onions, chopped finely

2 tbsp olive oil

2 tsp bouillon powder, gluten-free

4 garlic cloves, minced

2 tsp tomato purée

1 x 400ml tomato sauce either tinned or glass jarred

3 tsp sun-dried tomato paste

mixed herbs

sea salt and cracked black pepper

garnish

6 large courgettes, made into spirals

parmesan cheese, grated

½ tbsp extra virgin olive oil (if sautéing the courgette spirals)

sea salt and cracked black pepper

Preparation time - 40 mins, cooking time - 50 mins

Add the olive oil to a large non-stick frying pan over a medium/high heat and fry. Fry the onions until translucent.

Add the cubed aubergines, and continue sautéing for a further 10 minutes until the aubergine starts to soften up.

Add the bouillon powder to the frying pan and continue to cook for a further 10 minutes. You will notice that the powder will draw the moisture from the aubergines.

Add the crushed garlic, black pepper and a little sea salt. Continue to sauté.

Reduce the heat then add the tomato purée and sun-dried tomato paste.

Add the tomato sauce, increase the heat until bubbling (continue stirring) then reduce to simmer and leave to cook for 30 minutes.

If your sauce reduces too much, you can add a little water.

Spiralise the courgette and either serve raw or you can Pan fry in ½ tbsp virgin olive oil, seasoned with sea salt and black pepper for 2 to 3 minutes.

Serve immediately sprinkled with grated parmesan and black pepper.

LISA'S TIP

If you don't have a spiraliser you can serve this sauce with your choice of gluten-free pasta. Or, if you prefer, try it cold with a variety of dips and gluten-free crackers!

Horseradish Mashed Potato

An elegant accompaniment to
meat, poultry, game or fish.

....

{serves 4 - 6}

ingredients

1 kilo Maris Piper potatoes, approx.
4 or 5 large ones

3-4 tbsp olive oil

1 tbsp horseradish cream

sea salt and white pepper

Preparation time - 20 mins, cooking time - 30 mins

Peel your potatoes and cut into quarters and place in a saucepan with cold salted water and bring to the boil. Boil the potatoes for 20 mins until soft. Check with a knife that they are ready, then drain.

Next place a sieve over a bowl and squeeze your potatoes through the sieve or a potato ricer to remove any lumps and bumps.

Add your coconut or olive oil and season with sea salt & white pepper.

Finally add your horseradish cream, give a good stir.

LISA'S TIP

Why don't you try piping out the mashed potatoes through a piping bag with a fluted nozzle? Such a fun way to serve individual portions of mashed taters! If you are so inclined, you can make these ahead of time up to the point of piping them out. Just cover them and set in the refrigerator until you are ready then bake to re-heat before serving.

Soups & Sides

Lamb Tagine with Prunes, Almonds & Dates

An ideal dish for a family gathering. Consider a crunchy chopped salad of shredded carrots, onions, red cabbage, cucumber and ruby red pomegranate drizzled with olive oil and seasoned with sea salt, cracked pepper and lemon to accompany.

....

{serves 4 - 6}

ingredients

1.5kg lamb shoulder, deboned, well-trimmed, cut in 3cm cubes

2 tbsp olive oil

1 onion, finely chopped

1 red onion, finely chopped

2 garlic cloves, minced

50g blanched almonds

1 x 400g tin chickpeas, drained

1 cinnamon stick

250g pitted prunes

70g pitted dates, chopped

2 tbsp honey, agave nectar or maple syrup

1 x 400g tin plum tomatoes, sieved to discard the seeds

2 tbsp Osem brand onion soup mix dissolved in 250-300ml boiling water

50ml pomegranate concentrate dissolved with 50ml boiling water

sea salt and freshly ground black pepper

1 tsp garlic granules

1 tsp paprika

1 tsp ground ginger

1 tsp ground coriander

2 tsp cinnamon

garnish

fresh coriander, a small bunch

serve with quinoa or wholegrain rice

Preparation time - 40 mins, cooking time - 1.5 to 2hrs

Preheat the oven to 325°F, gas mark 3, 180°C (160°C fan-assisted)

Place your casserole dish over the stove, gently heat the olive oil, and sauté the finely chopped onions until translucent.

Decant the onions to a mixing bowl.

In a separate large mixing bowl, add ground ginger, coriander, cinnamon, paprika, garlic granules, sea salt and black pepper.

Place the casserole dish back on the stove and seal the lamb for 5 minutes, then spoon the lamb into the mixing bowl with the seasoning.

Coat the lamb in the seasoning then set aside.

Pour the sautéed onions back into the casserole dish on the heat, add the crushed garlic and sauté for a further 5 minutes.

Add the chopped dates, prunes and almonds to the onions.

Pour in the dissolved pomegranate concentrate, onion soup mix and then add the seasoned lamb with the cinnamon stick, cook for a further 2 minutes.

Sieve the canned plum tomatoes, discarding the seeds. Place the juice of the tomatoes into a small mixing bowl, add the honey (or preferred choice), combine together then pour over the lamb.

Bring the liquid to the boil, then reduce to medium/low heat.

Cover with a lid and place in the preheated oven and cook gently for 1.5-2 hours, check every 30 minutes.

After 1 hour, add the chick peas, continue cooking and reduce the oven temperature to 300°F, gas mark 2, 160°C (140°C fan-assisted).

Serve immediately with quinoa or wholegrain rice.

LISA'S TIP

Prepare then place in the oven and spend time with your guests before serving! This dish is so comforting. The dates and honey give a natural sweetness.

Chicken Tagine with Apricots & Ginger

For modern cooks, a tagine is low-and-slow stewing, with very little fat or liquid. The Moroccan, Tunisian and Algerian dishes that form the basis of tagine cuisine feature an abundance of 'warm spices' -- cinnamon, cumin, coriander -- along with garlic, onion and sometimes lemon.

{serves 4 - 6}

ingredients

8 chicken thighs

2 tbsp olive oil

1 onion, finely chopped

1 tbsp ginger, peeled and grated

1-2 (depending on preference) red chillies, deseeded and finely chopped

1 cinnamon stick

250g ready to eat dried apricots

2 tbsp honey, agave nectar or maple syrup

1 x 400g tin plum tomatoes, sieve and discard the seeds

2 tbsp Osem brand onion soup mix

200-250ml boiling water

sea salt and cracked black pepper

paprika

garlic granules

garnish

1 handful fresh coriander

quinoa, cooked

Preparation time - 30 mins, cooking time - 1.5 to 2hrs

Preheat the oven to 400°F, gas mark 6, 200°C (180°C fan-assisted)

Rinse off the chicken under cold water and remove any stray feathers by scraping with the blade of a knife.

Place a large non-stick frying pan on the stove, together with a splash of olive oil when the pan is hot, place the chicken in the pan and seal for approximately 2 minutes on each side until golden, then remove from the heat.

When the chicken has cooled down, season with a little sea salt, black pepper, paprika and garlic granules.

Place your casserole dish over the stove, gently heat the olive oil, and sauté the finely chopped onion until translucent.

Turn the heat down, add the chillies and grated ginger and cook for a further 2 minutes.

Add the apricots together with the cinnamon stick and continue to cook again for a further 2 minutes.

Dissolve the onion soup mix in 200ml boiling water, then pour into the casserole dish (You may need an extra 50ml of water once the chicken has been added, to ensure there is enough liquid to cover the base of the casserole dish and submerge the apricots).

Add the seasoned chicken thighs and carefully baste over the juices.

Sieve the canned plum tomatoes and discard the seeds into a small mixing bowl. Add the honey (or preferred choice), combine together then pour over the chicken.

Bring the liquid to the boil, then reduce to medium/low heat.

Cover with a lid and place in the preheated oven and cook gently for 1.5-2 hours, check every 30 minutes.

Garnish with fresh coriander and serve with plain cooked quinoa.

LISA'S TIP

The advantage of this recipe is that you don't need a tagine or lots of time. After getting the apricots simmering, toss everything except the coriander into the casserole dish. After 1.5-2 hours in the oven, it is ready to serve on a bed of quinoa.

Aubergine & Autumn Vegetable Curry

Seek out small, slender aubergines for this recipe. With less seeds, they tend to be less bitter and become tender and sweet when cooked.

{serves 4 - 6}

ingredients

2 aubergines, medium, cut into 1.5cm cubes

1 butternut squash, cut into 1.5cm cubes

2 sweet potatoes, cut into 1.5cm cubes

2 carrots, cut into 1.5 inch rounds

1 red onion, small, sliced into half moons

1 white onion, small, sliced into half moons

1 tin butter beans, drained

400ml organic coconut milk (canned)

300g tomato pasta sauce (smooth as possible)

½ litre vegetable stock, gluten-free

3 garlic cloves, minced

2 tsp mild madras curry powder

2 tsp coconut sugar

2 tbsp coconut oil (virgin or odourless)

sea salt & black pepper

garnish

wholegrain rice
1 handful fresh coriander, chopped

Preparation time - 40 mins, cooking time - 2 hours

Preheat the oven to 400°F, gas mark 6, 200°C (180°C fan-assisted).

Heat the oil in a large (29cm diameter) casserole dish on medium heat.

Add the onions and sauté until translucent (approx. 5 minutes).

Add the aubergines, salt, pepper, tomato sauce and crushed garlic, mix well and cook for 2-3 minutes longer.

Add the remaining vegetables: butternut squash, sweet potatoes, carrots and butterbeans

Pour over the vegetable stock, followed by the coconut milk, keep on the stove for another 2-4 minutes until the stew comes to a boil.

Add the curry powder and coconut sugar.

Cover the pot and place in the centre of the oven for two hours. Check every 30 minutes and stir to ensure nothing gets stuck to the base of the dish. If you would like to keep the dish in the oven after two hours reduce the oven temperature to 300°F, gas mark 2, 150°C (130°C fan-assisted).

Serve with wholegrain rice & freshly chopped coriander.

LISA'S TIP

Sweet potatoes are packed with beta-carotene and antioxidants. In fact, they have more beta-carotene than carrots! They also contain vitamins C, E, folate, thiamine, riboflavin, fibre and several minerals. Because of their lower glycemic index, they are a carbohydrate-friendly choice, too.

Bolognese with Spiralised Sweet Potato

My version of 'spag bol', this meat and potatoes dish is
deliciously filling and nutritionally balanced.

....

{serves 4 - 6}

ingredients

500g lean minced beef

2 echalions shallots or white
onions, finely chopped

120g button mushrooms, cut into
small cubes

2 x 400g cans plum tomatoes,
sieved (discard the pulp and pips)

Small handful of basil or dried
mixed herbs

2 tbsp olive oil

2 tbsp tomato purée

2 tsp Worcestershire sauce or
tamari soy sauce, gluten-free

2 tsp honey, agave nectar or
maple syrup

3 garlic cloves, minced

150ml white wine

garlic granules

sea salt and cracked black pepper

garnish

4 large sweet potatoes

olive oil

parmesan cheese or dairy free
cheese, grated

sprigs of basil

Preparation time - 40 mins, cooking time - 45 to 60 mins

Heat a large non-stick saucepan or flame-proof casserole dish over a
high heat, then add the oil together with the shallots or onions and
sauté until soft and translucent (approx. 3 mins).

Remove the pan from the heat. Add the crushed garlic and
Worcestershire sauce. Coat the onions well then add the minced
beef in several batches until the onions are blended into the meat.

Return to the heat and continue to stir over a medium/high heat
until browned. Break up any lumps with the back of a wooden
spoon. At this point, the mince will have changed colour from pink
to grey, to golden brown.

Add the mushrooms and continue to stir for 3 minutes then add the
tomato purée.

Make a well in the centre and pour in the wine. Continue to stir for
3 minutes until the wine has evaporated.

Add the basil leaves, if using, or add dried herbs, then pour over the
tomato sauce and season with sea salt, black pepper, garlic granules
and honey (or preferred choice).

Partly cover the pan, then simmer on a low light for 45-60 minutes
until the mince is tender and surrounded with a rich thick sauce
(stir every 10 minutes).

Taste to check seasoning. Add sea salt and black pepper if necessary
and once cooked, set aside.

Peel the sweet potatoes and spiralise to get sweet potato pasta.

Place the sweet potato pasta in a large wok/frying pan with a drizzle
of olive oil and sauté for 3-4 minutes to lightly soften.

The spiralised pasta should have a bite to it so be sure not to overcook.

When you're ready to serve, heat up the sauce.

Garnish with basil and a sprinkle of parmesan cheese or vegan
cheese if dairy free.

LISA'S TIP

*This meat sauce is a good recipe to freeze up to 3 months. Defrost
thoroughly, then return to a saucepan and reheat gently, bubble for 10
minutes and use in other recipes.*

Autumnal Macarons

Macarons have a smoother texture than the ones found in traditional bakeries and often feature a filling. I've suggested dates or chestnuts.

....

{makes 22}

ingredients

125g almond meal
150g pure icing sugar
100g egg whites (approx. 3 eggs)
60g caster sugar
natural yellow colouring gel

choice of fillings

150g dates (stones removed)
8 tbsp almond milk
sea salt, pinch
or
150g chestnut spread, vanilla
8 tbsp almond milk
sea salt, pinch

Preparation time - 2 hours, cooking time - 20 to 25 mins

Preheat the oven to 375°F, gas mark 5, 190°C (170°C fan-assisted).

Line baking trays with double sheets of baking paper or use a silicone or macaron mat. Sift almond meal and icing sugar together; sift mixture twice more, then set aside. Beat egg whites until foamy; add your food colouring at this point. Continue beating on low speed, adding coconut sugar a tbsp at a time. Increase to high speed and beat until mixture forms glossy, stiff peaks. Fold in half the almond meal mixture. Repeat with second half. Using your spoon or spatula, swipe the mixture against the side of the bowl. Then scoop the batter from the bottom and plop it upside-down. This movement deflates the meringue. Repeat process until batter is runny, shiny and slowly slides the sides. Test by plopping a teaspoon of batter on a small plate. If the peak sinks back into the batter within 15 seconds, it is done.

Fill a piping bag with a 1cm round nozzle and pipe rounds of batter onto your baking trays. Now, bang your trays against the counter to knock any air out of the batter. Set aside to dry at room temperature for 45mins - 1 hour.

Place tray in the oven, reduce temperature to 140°C (120°C fan-assisted) and bake for 20-25 minutes. Watch that your macarons don't burn. They are ready when they can be lifted from the baking paper without sticking. Mine usually take 23 minutes but this may vary.

To make the date or chestnut filling, place the dates or chestnut spread in a mini food processor blend until smooth and then add the almond milk and pinch of sea salt blending until smooth. Place the filling on one macaron then cover with another one.

Heaven.

LISA'S TIP
Every baker has an opinion about the best way to create the perfect macaron batter, a process known as macaronnage. The idea is to press out just enough air from the batter so that it runs off your spatula thickly, slowly, but consistently.

Apple & Almond Pudding

Comfort food can look appealing, too. Prepare in ramekins
and serve individually for a more sophisticated look.

....

{makes 22}

ingredients

700g cooking apples, cored, peeled
and roughly chopped

150ml water, just enough to cover
the apples)

2 tbsp honey, depending on the
sharpness of the apples

120g coconut sugar

120g ground almonds, sieved

120g margarine

2 large eggs, beaten.

garnish

coconut yoghurt (coyo)

Preparation time - 30 mins, cooking time - 30 to 40 mins

Preheat the oven to 375°F, gas mark 5, 180°C (160°C fan-assisted).

Core, peel and roughly chop the cooking apples.

Place in a saucepan with approximately 150ml water, just enough
to cover the apples, together with 2 tbsp honey (depending on the
sharpness of the apples).

Bring to a boil then cook on a low heat until the apples are stewed,
approx 10 minutes.

Remove from heat and allow to cool for 10 minutes, then transfer
into an 18cm Pyrex bowl.

Using an electric mixer or by hand, cream the margarine and
coconut sugar until pale and fluffy. Then beat in the eggs a little at
a time.

When both eggs are incorporated, carefully and lightly fold in the
sieved ground almonds.

Bake on a middle shelf for 30-40 minutes.

Sieve hot or cold with coconut yoghurt.

LISA'S TIP

*Can also be served with banana ice cream. Once cooled, it will keep
in the fridge for up to 4 days. You can also try different variations of
fruits: rhubarb, plum, peaches, apricot or pear! This is a perfect dessert
for guests who are wheat or gluten intolerant.*

Raw Chocolate Brownies

Made with whole food ingredients, these
divine brownies are truly indulgent.

{makes 22}

ingredients

250g rolled jumbo oats, gluten-free

500g Medjool soft dates, pitted
(pre-soak if hard)

25g raw cacao powder

½ tsp vanilla bean extract or ½
vanilla pod, deseeded

1/4 tsp sea salt, crushed

100g dark chocolate chips (or you
can use milk chocolate chips if no
dairy allergies)

chocolate coating

160g coconut oil (virgin or
odourless), melted and leave
to cool

120g agave nectar or maple syrup

80g raw cacao powder

sea salt

1 tsp vanilla bean extract or 1
vanilla pod, deseeded

Preparation time - 30 mins, freeze time - 60 mins (plus refrigeration)

Line a 23cm square pan with parchment paper.

In a food processor, process the oats into a fine sandy consistency, with a slight rough texture, then take them out.

Place the pitted dates in the food processor and process until finely chopped and smooth, then add the grounded oats, cacao powder, vanilla and sea salt and process until thoroughly combined, keep scraping down the sides and breaking up the mixture.

When the mixture has formed into a log or ball shape remove from the food processor and place in your pre-lined tin.

I wear disposable gloves at this point to evenly press the mixture into the prepared square pan until smooth, or you can use the back of a large spoon.

Then scatter over the chocolate chips and then press into the mixture.

Place in the freezer for about 10 minutes.

For the chocolate topping, add the agave nectar (or preferred choice) to the coconut oil and add in the salt and vanilla and whisk in the cacao powder until smooth.

Remove the brownies from the freezer and pour on the chocolate topping and spread out evenly.

Carefully transfer the pan to the freezer on a flat even surface and chill for 50 minutes until the topping is firm enough to slice.

Run hot water over a knife for a minute or so, wipe quickly with a towel, and carefully slide the knife into the brownies to slice (warming up the knife helps it slice more evenly without much cracking).

Store leftovers in the fridge for a chocolate treat anytime!

Invite friends round to share!

LISA'S TIP

You have to keep these brownies either in the freezer or fridge to prevent the topping from melting, however remove from the fridge or freezer 30 minutes before serving. My advice would be, once made, cut into squares and keep on a flat platter covered with cling film in the fridge.

Fig & Almond Cake

This is a light cake that's rich and buttery on the bottom. An ideal treat that has the health benefits of almonds and figs.

{serves 10 - 12}

ingredients

3-4 fresh figs, sliced thinly (remove base and stalk)

4 large eggs

228g margarine

228g coconut sugar

228g ground almonds, sifted

½ tsp almond extract

topping

20g flaked almonds, toasted

2 tbsp apricot or strawberry jam (sugar free)

Preparation time - 20 mins - Cooking time - 45 mins

Preheat the oven to 375°C, gas mark 5, 180°C (160°C fan-assisted).

Line the base and side of a non-stick loose bottom, 20cm springform tin with parchment paper.

Place the sliced figs around the base of the tin.

In an electric mixer or by hand, cream the margarine and coconut sugar until pale and fluffy. Now beat in the eggs a little at a time.

Add the almond extract and then lightly fold in the sieved ground almonds.

Spread this mixture carefully over the figs, and even out the surface with the back of a tablespoon.

Then bake on a middle shelf in the oven for exactly 45 minutes.

Remove from the oven and leave to cool over a wire rack.

When cooled, loosen the mixture around the edges.

Place a serving plate over the tin and flip over, then release the clasp.

Peel away the parchment paper.

For the apricot or strawberry glaze: heat the jam in a small saucepan over a medium heat until liquid (melted). You can add a touch of water if the consistency is too thick. Then remove from heat and strain the jam through a fine strainer to remove any fruit lumps, let cool until it is only slightly warm, then using a pastry brush glaze the tart.

Sprinkle with toasted almonds.

Serve with ice cream or coconut yogurt.

LISA'S TIP

The cake itself is simple to make and very good! Consider also using apricots or peaches instead of figs. Store in an airtight container in the fridge for up to 5 days. Bring to room temperature before serving.

WINTER

seasonal moods

Diffused light makes our landscapes softer and if it snows, there's a quiet like no other time. Our tendency is to run from work to home, escaping the cold and rushing inside, but when there's a clear winter day, there are few things more beautiful. We just have to remember to look!

Whilst the trees might be bare of their leaves, the ground is active. Now is when root vegetables are at their peak: celeriac with its distinctive flavour and versatile uses; sensational beetroot with its sultry red colour and taste; and Jerusalem artichokes which add a nutty flavour to soups. Brussels sprouts, when prepared with love and time, are surprisingly delicious as is spinach, perhaps flavoured with lemon, a taste of forgotten sun.

The trick now is to think less hibernating bear and more snow mink! Inside the house – and perhaps just a little too close to the kitchen – temptations are plenty. Use the weather to your advantage and keep your house full of delicious, attractive choices in brilliant colours. Make larger quantities of soups, stews and casseroles to share - after all, what's really better than providing healthy, nourishing foods to those we love?

BEETROOT The Romans praised its medicinal and aphrodisiac qualities, but beetroots are a new superfood because of an abundance of potassium and magnesium. Roast them for an added depth of flavour.

JERUSALEM ARTICHOKE Related to the sunflower and not a true artichoke, this oddly named tuber has a sweet, nutty flavour. Traditionally used in soups, it is high in iron and vitamin C. But, beware, it does have a property similar to baked beans!

PISTACHIOS With fewer calories than the average nut, pistachios are also a rich source for potassium and vitamin K. Grown in dry Mediterranean climates and recently cultivated in California, pistachios can be used in both sweet and savoury dishes.

SPINACH Belonging to the food group family that also includes beetroot, chard and quinoa, spinach has an impressive array of health benefits. It contains vitamin C, vitamin E, beta-carotene, manganese, zinc and selenium. Try steamed, sautéed or raw in salads.

CARROTS While seeing in the dark is a myth, carrots do contain the highest level of vitamin A found in a vegetable. Try tossing them in cider vinegar for an energising salad or, like other root vegetables, they benefit from roasting.

LEMON Natural vitamin C is much more effective than synthetic, so reduce your chances of catching a cold by drinking some fresh lemon juice diluted in water every day. Try hot water with a touch of honey and lemon for a refreshingly warm variation.

CELERIAC A singularly unattractive vegetable, celeriac is ideal for low-carbohydrate diets. Chip, mash or grate for a huge variety of delicious variations. A French-staple which is slowly making its way into mainstream meals, celeriac takes like a cross between potatoes and celery.

BRUSSELS SPROUTS One of the world's healthiest foods (really!), this edible bud packs in over 100% of your daily requirement of vitamin C. Low in fat and sodium the mighty sprout needs a delicate hand. Try cutting them in half, blanching, then tossing in olive oil and garlic. Delicious!

Omelette with Avocado & Sunkissed Tomato

A quick, nutritious breakfast that also works well in the
evening with a green salad and a glass of wine!

{serves 2}

ingredients

6 eggs
2 tbsp rapeseed oil
sea salt and white pepper

garnish

1 avocado, cut each half in six slices
1 medium tomato, cut into 6 wedges
8 sunkissed tomatoes
1 handful fresh coriander, chopped
balsamic, drizzle
olive oil
cracked black pepper
sea salt

Preparation time - 15 mins, cooking time - 3 mins per omelette

To cook the omelette, preheat a 7cm non-stick pan over a medium/high heat.

Beat the eggs with a fork until they are well blended with no streaks of egg white. Season with sea salt and white pepper.

Add the rapeseed oil to the pan, once melted, turn the heat down to medium.

Add the eggs and scramble with a heat-resistant spatula. Once the eggs begin to set a bit, shake the pan back and forth while still scrambling, so the runny egg fills any gaps or holes on the bottom.

Once the egg has almost set, turn down the heat to medium/low and evenly smooth out.

Now slide onto a serving plate, top with avocado slices, tomato wedges, sunkissed tomatoes and chopped coriander.

Season with sea salt and cracked black pepper.

Lightly drizzle with olive oil and balsamic.

Omelettes are very filling although you can serve with some gluten-free bread to mop up any juices!

LISA'S TIP

If you prefer you can add filling directly onto the omelette in the pan. The number one rule is not to over-mix – no beating or whisking. Practice with plain omelettes before you try filling. Don't put too much inside; it gets difficult to fold the omelette over. You can always put more filling on top.

Green Goddess Smoothie

This Green Goddess smoothie is great for balancing sugar cravings, uplifting the mood, clearing the head, boosting metabolism and strengthening immunity.

....

{serves 2}

ingredients

400ml apple juice

1 large banana, frozen if you prefer ice cold smoothies

1 kiwi

½ cucumber, peeled and cut into chunks

½ avocado

1 inch ginger, peeled and grated

1 large handful curly kale, stalks removed or spinach

1 bunch of fresh coriander

1 tbsp SuperLife Superfood smoothie mix

couple of ice cubes if you are using fresh bananas

garnish

cucumber slices

fresh coriander

Preparation time - 20 mins

Peel and slice: kiwi, avocado, cucumber and your banana if not already frozen.

Peel and grate the ginger finely.

In a blender combine the apple juice, banana, kiwi, avocado and cucumber and blend until smooth.

Add your ginger, curly kale or spinach and coriander and again thoroughly blend.

Add the SuperLife Superfood smoothie mix and ice cubes if required and give one more blend again until smooth.

Divide between two tall glasses or mason jars and serve right away, or you can keep refrigerated, for one day.

Drink and feel great.

LISA'S TIP

SuperLife Smoothie Mix is a combination of eight raw superfoods that gives you an energy boost for the entire day.
1. Hemp - rich in protein and omega-3s
2. Maca - for energy, focus & memory, and an aphrodisiac
3. Lucuma - balances sugar levels for lasting energy
4. Cacao - high in magnesium, energy & mood booster
5. Spirulina - anti-inflammatory, strengthens the joints
6. Chlorella - strengthens immune system, helps remove toxins
7. Kelp - high in iodine, balances thyroid
8. Barley Grass - high in chlorophyll, alkalizes the body, helps with weight loss

Eggs Baked in Portobello Mushrooms

This breakfast dish can also be served with rocket and
sunkissed tomatoes for a lunchtime treat.

{serves 4}

ingredients

4 portobello mushrooms, insides
scraped and stalks removed

4 eggs, medium

1 tsp olive oil

4 tbsp grated mozzarella

3 tbsp finely grated parmesan
cheese

sea salt and cracked black pepper

garnish

2 avocados, cubed

3-4 medium tomatoes, deseeded
and chopped into chunks

1-2 tbsp sweet chilli sauce

1 tbsp olive oil

1 handful fresh coriander, chopped

chives, chopped

cracked black pepper

Preparation time - 20 mins, cooking time - 14 to 15 mins

Preheat the oven to 350°F, gas mark 4, 180°C (160°C fan-assisted).

Line a baking tray with a silicone baking mat or parchment paper.

Clean the mushrooms with a mushroom brush.

Carefully cut out the stalk, then with a teaspoon scoop out the gills
of each portobello mushroom cap. This will give you extra room
and prevent your mushroom from being too watery.

Place the mushrooms on the baking tray, drizzle a teaspoon of olive
oil, then season with a little sea salt and black pepper.

In a separate small bowl crack each egg then pour into the
mushroom cap.

Sprinkle a little pinch of sea salt over the egg, 1 tbsp of mozzarella
around the white of the egg, and scatter over the parmesan cheese,
leaving some of the yolk exposed.

Bake in the preheated oven on the centre shelf for 14-15 minutes.

To make the avocado salsa, mix the cubed avocado, tomato and
season with sea salt, black pepper, olive oil, chopped coriander and
sweet chilli sauce.

Remove baked eggs from the oven and allow to set for about 3
minutes before serving.

Scatter the avocado & tomato salsa over the baked eggs and garnish
with chopped chives.

LISA'S TIP

*Since this recipe is so quick to pull together and packed with tons of
flavour and nutrition, you'll turn to it time and again.*

Homemade Granola

This homemade granola allows you to control the amount of sugar on your morning cereal. The freshly roasted nuts add flavour to a higher level, too!

{serves 12}

ingredients

400g gluten-free oats, sifted
60g sunflower seeds
60g pumpkin seeds
80g whole pecans
100g whole almonds
4 tbsp rice bran oil
8 tbsp honey, agave nectar or maple syrup
2 pinches sea salt
1 tsp vanilla bean extract

garnish

1 tbsp toasted sesame seeds
100g raisins
80g banana chips
20g coconut chips

Preparation time - 20 mins, cooking time - 15 to 20 mins

Preheat the oven to 400°F, gas mark 6, 200°C (180°C fan-assisted).

Cover a large baking tray with a silicone baking mat or parchment paper, add the sifted oats, whole almonds, whole pecans, sunflower and pumpkin seeds and spread in a even layer.

Bake in the preheated oven for 10 minutes, check every 5 minutes and stir to ensure the nuts don't over brown or burn.

Bake until crisp and golden.

In a small sauce pan heat the oil, maple syrup (or preferred choice), vanilla bean extract and salt over a gentle heat for 2 minutes, then set aside.

When the oat mixture has cooked, remove from the oven and pour over the maple syrup mixture, mix until well coated.

Place the granola back in the oven, cook for 5-10 minutes, stirring after 5 minutes.

Remove from the oven and leave to cool on the tray. Add the toasted sesame seeds, raisins, banana and coconut chips.

Serve with cold milk or yogurt.

The granola can be stored in an airtight container for up to a month.

LISA'S TIP

Serve on coconut yogurt, topped with granola and blueberries. You can be adventurous with your nuts and seeds. When cooked you can add an assortment of dried fruits. My preference is for dried banana chips and pecans, but once you get the hang of making your own, you really can be adventurous!

Roasted Beetroot & Orange Salad

Not only is this an attractive dish, the
'sugared' walnuts are addictive – beware!

{serves 4}

ingredients

720g beetroots (approx. 4 large beetroots), trimmed and scrubbed

3 large oranges, pith and peel removed and cut into segments (see Lisa's tip)

100g stilton cheese, crumbled

80g walnuts

boiling water

1 tbsp coconut sugar

3 tbsp olive oil

sea salt and cracked black pepper

garnish

rocket, chopped chives, coriander or parsley

Preparation time - 20 mins, cooking time - 1 hour plus cooling time

Preheat the oven to 400°F, gas mark 6, 200°C (180°C fan-assisted).

To roast the beetroots, if the leaves are still attached, cut them off, leaving 1 inch of the stem attached, scrub with cold water but do not peel. Place 4 squares of aluminium foil on a baking tray enough to cover the beetroots and make into a parcel. Placing the beetroot on each foil, lift the corners to cover, then divide 1 tbsp of extra virgin olive oil between the 4 parcels, wrap tightly, pinching the edges of the foil together. Place in the preheated oven for about 1 hour, or until tender when pierced with a thin knife or a skewer. When fully roasted, remove and carefully open the foil packet. Let the beetroots stand until cool enough to handle. Wearing rubber gloves, place the beetroot in your hand and carefully peel off the outer layer. Cut the beetroots in chunky slices, place in a mixing bowl and season with sea salt and cracked black pepper, drizzle with 2 tbsp extra virgin olive oil.

Bring a small saucepan of water to the boil, add the walnuts and boil for 2 minutes, then strain through a sieve. Place the walnuts on a baking tray pre-lined with a silicone baking mat or parchment paper and toss the nuts in coconut sugar. Bake in the oven for 8-10 minutes. Segment the oranges (see Lisa's tip).

Place the beetroots on a serving platter, again using rubber gloves, then top with the orange segments, crumbled stilton cheese and toasted sugared walnuts. If you desire, drizzle with olive oil and season with a little sea salt and black pepper. Garnish with some rocket, chopped chives, coriander or parsley.

LISA'S TIP

The trick to segmenting oranges is to cut the ends off an orange just far enough to expose the flesh, then place the orange cut end down, and cut away as little of the peel as possible by following the orange's shape. Using a sharp knife cut along the inside of the membranes that separate the orange segments, slice only down to the centre of the orange, continue around the entire orange cutting out each section, leaving the membrane.

Courgette & Shiitake Mushroom Quinoa Frittata

Frittatas are Italian, open-faced omelettes traditionally started on the stove and finished under the grill. Use any combination of vegetables for good results.

....

{serves 8 - 10}

ingredients

150g quinoa

250ml cold water

300g shiitake mushrooms, sliced

6 large eggs, beaten

2 courgettes, grated

2 tbsp rapeseed oil

150g grated cheddar cheese

2 tbsp honey, agave nectar or maple syrup

2 tbsp tamari soy sauce, gluten-free

sea salt and white pepper

Preparation time - 30 mins, cooking time - 55 to 60 mins

Preheat the oven to 350°F, gas mark 4, 180°C (160°C fan-assisted).

Line the base and sides of a 23cm non-stick springform tin with parchment paper.

Place the quinoa in a sieve and rinse until the water runs clear. Place in a medium saucepan with 250ml cold water and bring to a boil. Cover and simmer for 15 minutes, then take off the heat and leave to cool.

In a frying pan, add the rapeseed oil and sauté the sliced mushrooms until soft. Now add the tamari soy sauce and honey (or preferred choice), and continue to cook for 5 minutes. Leave to cool.

In a large mixing bowl, add the eggs and beat well, season with sea salt and white pepper.

Add the grated courgette, grated cheese, quinoa and mushrooms and mix well.

Place the tin over a tray with a rack underneath to prevent any leakage from the tin. Pour the mixture into the prepared tin.

Cover with foil and bake for 30 minutes, then remove the foil and bake for a further 20 minutes uncovered until golden and crisp. You might need an extra 5 minutes.

Leave to cool then release the side of the tine and you're ready to serve!

LISA'S TIP

This recipe is so versatile and perfect for picnics or lunches on the move. I tend to have one of these quinoa frittata cakes sitting in my fridge each week as a slice is a healthy snack between meals. This recipe contains fresh courgettes, shiitake mushrooms and cheddar cheese, because that's what I had in the fridge, but I can think of a million different combos that would be equally delish; broccoli & cheddar, sundried tomato & pesto, butternut squash & feta, or grated sweet potato & courgette, just don't forget to add the honey and soy to this combination. The possibilities are endless!

Moroccan Carrot & Chickpea Quinoa Salad

If you want even more Morocccan flavour, add cumin to the
quinoa when cooking or rosewater to the cooled dish.

{serves 6 - 8}

ingredients

240g quinoa, mixed red and white

4 carrots, grated

100g raisins

1 tsp olive oil

1 tsp cinnamon

2 tsp honey, agave nectar or maple syrup

½ litre boiling water

120g chickpeas, rinsed

2 handfuls coriander, chopped

2 ½ tbsp. olive oil

3 tsp lemon juice

sea salt and cracked black pepper

paprika

garnish

20g crushed pistachios

35g pine nuts, toasted

fresh coriander to taste or flat-leaf parsley

Preparation time - 30 mins, cooking time - 25 mins

Rinse the quinoa and set aside.

In a medium saucepan add ½ tbsp of olive oil and then add the grated carrots and raisins and sauté over a gentle heat.

Add the quinoa, cinnamon and honey (or preferred choice), then stir until thoroughly combined.

Add the boiling water, bring back to the boil, then cover. Reduce the heat to a simmer and cook for 20 minutes. Remove from the heat and let the mixture rest for a further 5 minutes.

Fluff with a fork then leave to cool.

Toast the pine nuts in a non-stick pan over a medium heat until browned.

In a large mixing bowl add: 2 tbsp olive oil, lemon juice, chickpeas, coriander, sea salt, black pepper and paprika.

When the quinoa has fully cooled, fold it into the mixture in the large mixing bowl.

Scatter with toasted pine nuts and crushed pistachios.

Garnish with freshly chopped coriander or flat-leaf parsley.

LISA'S TIP

Sometimes 'cupboard cooking' yields fantastic results. This recipe was invented when I needed to use up a bunch of fresh herbs and some canned chickpeas I had on hand. Now my family requests the dish! This salad will keep for a few days in the fridge, during which time the flavours can often improve.

Petit Pois, Avocado & Crispy Curly Kale Salad

Striking colours and bold flavours
makes this salad a real winner!

....

{serves 4-6}

ingredients

300g petit pois, frozen (thawed)

100g curly kale

2 avocados, cut into small cubes

300g beetroots, rinse under water before roasting leave the skin on

4 tbsp olive oil

bunch of chives

sea salt and cracked black pepper

chilli flakes

4 tbsp olive oil

dressing

100ml extra virgin olive oil

20ml white wine vinegar

25ml balsamic vinegar

1tsp Dijon honey mustard

1¼ tbsp. honey, agave nectar or maple syrup

sea salt and cracked black pepper

Preparation time - 60 mins, cooking time - 30 mins

Preheat the oven to 375°F, gas mark 5, 190°C (170°C fan-assisted).

Remove the petit pois from the freezer and leave in a bowl to thaw out.

Make the dressing by mixing together with a small whisk: extra virgin olive oil, white wine vinegar, balsamic, Dijon honey mustard, honey (or preferred choice), sea salt and black pepper.

Place each beetroots on individual large squares of foil. Pick up the sides and meet at the top to create a parcel. Drizzle inside each parcel with olive oil and season with sea salt, cracked black pepper and chilli flakes.

Close the parcels and place on a baking tray, bake for 1 hour until soft.

Remove from oven and leave to cool. Once completely cooled, gently rub off the skins (best to wear disposable gloves). Cut into small cubes, then pour 2 tbsp of the dressing over the beetroot and leave to marinade.

Line a baking tray with parchment paper. Place the curly kale on the tray and drizzle olive oil over the leaves, add a sprinkle of black pepper and sea salt and toss to coat completely.

Bake the kale in the pre-heated oven until the edges are brown but not burnt, about 12-15 minutes.

You can take the tray out after 5 minutes and turn over the leaves with a spatula if the edges are browning too quickly. It is done when the kale is crispy, not soft.

In a mixing bowl, add the petit pois, avocado and chopped chives. Lightly stir together, then place on a large serving platter and drizzle with 1 tbsp of the dressing.

Using gloves, carefully place the cubed beetroot over the peas and avocado, reserving any juices. Top the salad with the crispy, curly kale.

Drizzle any juices from the beetroot around the plate.

LISA'S TIP

Kale is one of the most nutritionally rich vegetables grown in Britain and with its curly leaves it's also one of the most attractive. So it's a mystery as to why it remains so underused by today's consumers. Don't miss out on this delicious 'superfood' - try it today!

Salmon with Wasabi Mayonnaise & Pistachio Crust

A quick, mid-week meal or formal enough for a dinner party,
this dish works well with a cucumber and dill salad.

{serves 4}

ingredients

4 salmon fillets, approx. 550g
(with skin)

1 tsp sesame oil

½ tbsp. rapeseed oil

1 tbsp mayonnaise

½ tsp wasabi powder/paste

40g roughly chopped pistachios

sea salt and cracked black pepper

Preparation time - 20 mins, cooking time - 10 to 12 mins (15 minutes if well cooked)

Preheat the oven to 400°F, gas mark 6, 200°C (180°C for fan-assisted).
Wash and pat dry the salmon fillets.

In a large non-stick frying pan, heat the rapeseed and sesame oil and place the salmon fillets in the pan, flesh side down, for 20 seconds.

Turn the fillets over on the skin side and cook for 2 minutes over a medium high heat. Take off the heat and allow to cool.

Once cooled, season the fillets with salt and cracked black pepper.

Mix: 1 tbsp mayonnaise with ½ tsp of wasabi powder or paste.

Place the fillets on a greased baking tray or dish, or if your frying pan can go in the oven, then use the same frying pan.

Using a knife, spread the mayonnaise mixture evenly over the top of the four fillets.

Press the chopped pistachios onto the top of each fillet covering completely.

Bake the salmon until cooked through and the crumb topping is crisp and golden brown, about 10-12 minutes (cook for 15 minutes if you prefer well cooked).

Using a large spatula, transfer salmon fillets onto a platter.

LISA'S TIP

It used to be seen as a luxury, but now salmon is one of the most popular oily fish consumed in the UK and why not when it's so versatile, readily available and is in season right now. If your pocket can afford it, wild salmon is worth seeking out rather than the farmed variety which can be fatty and tasteless. While many people find the stronger flavours of mackerel or sardines too much, salmon is a fantastic oily fish to include in your diet for wonderful health benefits.

Brussels Sprout Chips

Wait, don't turn the page – these chips are crispy, salty
and have an abundance of Vitamin C.

{serves 4 - 6}

ingredients

400g Brussels sprouts, stems
removed and leaves separated

10g parmesan cheese, grated

1 tbsp olive oil

sea salt and cracked black pepper

paprika

Preparation time - 20 mins, cooking time - 18 to 20 mins

Preheat the oven to 375°F, gas mark 5, 190°C (170°C fan-assisted).

Wash Brussels sprouts, trim the bottom stems and discard.

Remove any wilted outer leaves and discard.

Cut each sprout in half, remove loose leaves.

Combine halves and leaves in a bowl and toss with olive oil, sea salt, black pepper and paprika.

Pre-line a baking tray with a silicone baking mat or parchment paper and bake for 10 minutes, stirring every few minutes to prevent burning.

Now add the grated parmesan cheese and bake for a further 8-10 minutes.

LISA'S TIP

The easiest way to release the leaves is to keep trimming the bottom stem as you peel away the layers. This is the most time consuming part, but once it is done, the rest is a breeze. If you find peeling the layers off too time consuming, you can simply cut in half through the stem and roast the same way, although you might need to increase the cooking time by 5-10 minutes. Top the roasted Brussels sprout chips with extra parmesan and this is one addictive snack!

Borscht Soup

This soup from Eastern Europe has become trendy again. Perhaps more people are becoming aware of the health benefits of beets?

{serves 8 - 10}

ingredients

1.3kg large beetroots, peeled, skinned and cut into 3cm strips

1 large onion, sliced

2 celery stalks, cut into 3 pieces

2 carrots, cut in half lengthways and then into 3 pieces

2 tbsp vegetable oil

2 tbsp chicken stock powder, gluten-free

2 tbsp vegetable bouillon powder, gluten-free

2.25 litres water

2 tbsp honey, agave nectar or maple syrup

2 tbsp sushi seasoning vinegar

sea salt and white pepper

garnish

sour cream or coconut cream
fresh chopped dill leaves
whole beetroot from soup
grated hard boiled eggs
boiled potatoes

Preparation time - 30 mins, cooking time - 45 mins plus cooling and chilling time

Wearing gloves, trim the beetroots, wash then peel the skins and cut into 3cm strips, so you have thick matchstick pieces (try to cut into equal sizes, then you can use in a salad or as garnish).

Prepare the other vegetables as stated.

In a large saucepan on a high heat add the rapeseed oil and sauté the onions until soft.

Then add the carrots and celery and continue to sauté. Add the chicken and vegetable stock powder and keep stirring.

Remove from the heat and add the beetroot. Then place back on the heat and add a little over 2 litres of boiling water.

Season with sea salt and white pepper. Then add the honey (or preferred choice).

Bring to a boil, then cover loosely and continue to cook on a medium heat for 45 minutes.

After 45 minutes, remove from the heat and add the sushi seasoning vinegar.

Leave to cool completely for 3-4 hours.

Now place a large sieve over another large saucepan and strain through your soup.

Discard the celery stalk and carrot, keeping the beetroot for garnish.

Once the soup has cooled completely, place in the fridge until nice and cold.

When ready to serve, garnish with the reserved beetroot, chopped boiled eggs, boiled cubed potatoes, fresh dill leaves and coconut or sour cream.

LISA'S TIP

I used fresh beets from my local 'pick your own'. I love the deep ruby color of this borscht! It's so healthy and nutritious. It's as authentic as it gets. It can be served vegetarian style by omitting the chicken stock powder and doubling up on the bouillon.

Spicy Potatoes

Serve these spicy potatoes as part of an Indian buffet or liven
up your weekend roast with these crunchy firecrackers!

{serves 4-6}

ingredients

1.2kg Maris Piper potatoes

4 tbsp peanut or rapeseed oil

1 tsp black mustard seeds

1 tsp cumin seeds

½ tsp ground cumin

½ tsp sweet paprika

1 ½ tsp turmeric

¼ tsp chilli flakes

1 garlic clove, minced

2 tbsp lemon juice

sea salt

Preparation time - 30 mins, cooking time - 40 to 50 mins

Preheat the oven to 400°F, gas mark 6, 200°C (180°C fan-assisted).

Cut your potatoes in half, then quarter, then quarter each quarter
again and boil until just tender, approx. 10-12 mins. Rinse under cold
water, drain and cool.

Combine potatoes, oil, sea salt, seeds, spices, salt, garlic and lemon
juice in a baking dish.

Cook in a hot oven for about 30-40 minutes or until potatoes are nice
and crispy.

LISA'S TIP

*This recipe can be made 3 hours ahead. Store it, covered, in your
refrigerator. It can also be eaten cold. Just stir in 1 tbsp of coconut
cream with chopped coriander and 1 tbsp mango chutney for a
different style potato salad.*

Sweet Potato Hummus

An exciting version of this Middle Eastern dip
which also features pine nuts for crunch.

{serves 8 - 10}

ingredients

2 x 400g tins chickpeas in water,
drained

1 whole lemon

6-9 tbsp olive oil

4 tbsp raw tahini

3 garlic cloves, minced

4 tbsp water

sea salt

1 large sweet potato, roasted in skin

garnish

paprika

2 tbsp chickpeas, reserved from
ingredients

olive oil

pine nuts, toasted

parsley, Italian flat-leaf, roughly
chopped

Preparation time - 30 mins, cooking time - 50 to 60 minutes

Preheat the oven to 400°F, gas mark 6, 200°C (180°C fan-assisted).

Place the large sweet potato on a baking tray and bake for 50-60 minutes until soft, then remove from the oven and leave to cool.

Place the chickpeas in the food processor, reserving 2 tbsp for the garnish. Add 4 tbsp of tahini and process until smooth, occasionally wiping down the sides.

Add the crushed garlic, lemon juice, water, 6 tbsp olive olive oil and sea salt and process.

You may need to add the remaining 3 tbsp olive oil. Taste and adjust the seasoning.

If the paste is too thick, add 2-3 tbsp of water.

Scoop the inside of the sweet potato out of the skin and blend together with the chick peas until smooth.

To serve, place in serving dishes, using the back of a spoon create a well, drizzle with olive oil, sprinkle with the rest of the chickpeas, paprika, toasted pine nuts and chopped parsley.

LISA'S TIP

Hummus, the Arabic word for 'chickpeas', is relatively easy to make with the help of a blender and a few common, inexpensive ingredients. There are several brands of sesame tahini available and the one you choose can dramatically change the flavour of your hummus. Raw tahini can give your hummus a stronger and bitter flavour while canned, roasted tahini is mild and nutty.

Jerusalem Artichoke Soup

A good way to finally try those 'funny-looking' vegetables. A truly warming
and satisfying soup with the added bonus of a crispy parsnip topping.

{serves 4 - 6}

ingredients

1kg Jerusalem artichokes, peeled
and cut into 4 cm pieces

960ml boiling water

2 Echalion shallots, finely sliced (or
4 shallots)

2 tsp vegetable bouillon powder,
gluten-free

3 tbsp olive or rapeseed oil

2 cloves garlic, peeled

2 parsnips, peel and cut into 2 cm
pieces

1 tbsp coconut yogurt (if needed)

sea salt & white pepper

garnish

2 parsnips, peeled with vegetable
peeler

300ml rapeseed oil, for frying

sea salt

Preparation time - 30 mins, cooking time - 30 mins

Heat the oil in a heavy saucepan and sauté the finely sliced shallots
until translucent.

Add the garlic and sauté for one more minute continually stirring (be
careful not to burn the garlic).

Add the Jerusalem artichokes and parsnips and sauté for a few
minutes over a gentle heat.

Add the stock gradually, you may not need all of it, as Jerusalem
artichokes are very watery when cooked. Bring to the boil.

Season with sea salt and pepper, cover and cook for 30 minutes over a
low heat until the artichokes and parsnips are very tender.

Purée the soup in a food processor or using a hand stick blender.
Better yet, it is best to put through a blender so that you can gauge
the amount of liquid required. If using a hand blender, pour out some
liquid first (it's easier to add liquid then to remove it later).

Add the coconut yogurt (if needed), taste and adjust the seasoning.

Remove the skin of the parsnips, discard then continue peeling the
parsnips so you get strips of the length of parsnip.

Pre-heat the rapeseed oil in a medium deep saucepan. You will need
to fill the saucepan half-way with oil. In batches, drop in a handful of
the thinly sliced parsnips and as soon as the vegetable crisp starts to
change colour, remove from the hot oil using a slotted metal spoon.
Place on kitchen paper and sprinkle with some sea salt and repeat
with the remaining sliced parsnips.

Garnish the soup with the parsnip crisps.

LISA'S TIP

*If you'd like to make a Jerusalem artichoke risotto, keep the puréed
vegetables from the beginning stages and freeze to use when needed.*

Cottage Pie

There's a reason why this dish has remained a classic – it is incredibly satisfying. This version is dairy free.

{serves 4 - 6}

ingredients

4 potatoes (approx. 900g), cut into quarters

500g lean minced beef

2 Echalion shallots, finely chopped

1 tbsp tomato purée

3 tbsp tomato ketchup

2 tsp Worcestershire sauce, gluten-free

4 tbsp rapeseed oil

sea salt, white and cracked black pepper

garlic granules

Preparation time - 40 mins, cooking time - 30 mins

Preheat the oven to 375°F, gas mark 5, 190°C (170°C fan-assisted).

Put the potatoes in a large saucepan of lightly salted water and bring to the boil.

Reduce the heat slightly and simmer for 15-20 minutes until potatoes are soft.

Drain through a colander, then mash through a potato ricer directly back into the saucepan.

Season the potatoes lightly with sea salt and white pepper. Then mash in 2 tbsp of rapeseed oil over a gentle heat for 1 minute and set aside.

Heat the remaining oil in a non-stick frying pan, add the shallots and cook gently until translucent for 5 minutes or until soft.

Gradually add the minced beef, over a medium heat, breaking up with a wooden spoon, for 5 minutes until browned.

Add the tomato purée, tomato ketchup, Worcestershire sauce and season with garlic granules, sea salt and black pepper to taste.

Continue to cook over a low heat for 10 minutes.

Spoon the beef mixture into a 2 litre baking dish and carefully spoon the mash over the top, spreading over the surface of the filling.

Using a fork create a pattern over the top of the potato topping.

Bake in the preheated oven for 30 minutes, until heated through and the potato crust is golden.

LISA'S TIP

If you prefer more vegetables, add diced carrots and peas to the beef mixture. You can also substitute celeriac mash for the potatoes if you are trying to maintain a low-carb diet.

Hearty Beef Stew

A rich, satisfying dish that can be made several days ahead of time.
In fact, the flavours are better after a day or two in the fridge.

{serves 4}

ingredients

1kg boneless braising beef steak, cut into 5cm pieces

2 tbsp rapeseed oil

1 onion, finely chopped

1 red onion, finely chopped

3 garlic cloves, finely chopped

3 carrots, cut in half lengthways in diagonal 2.5cm pieces

2 celery sticks, cut into 2.5cm pieces

600g Maris Piper potatoes, cut into quarters (rinse under water to release starch)

1 sweet potato, cut into 2.5cm cubes

1 tbsp tomato ketchup

2 tsp Worcestershire sauce, gluten-free

200ml red wine

2 tbsp cornflour

1 bay leaf

850ml beef stock, gluten-free

sea salt and cracked black pepper

paprika

garlic granules

Preparation time - 30 mins, cooking time - 2.5 to 3 hours

Preheat the oven to 325°F, gas mark 3, 160°C (140°C fan-assisted).

In a mixing bowl combine the cornflour, paprika, garlic granules, sea salt and black pepper.

In a heavy based flameproof casserole dish (26cm in diameter), add 1 tbsp sunflower oil, brown the beef in batches for 3-4 minutes or until caramelised on all sides.

Then transfer to the mixing bowl and coat the beef in the seasoned corn flour, set aside.

Heat the remaining oil over a medium heat, add the onions to the casserole dish and cook until translucent for about 5 minutes.

Add the garlic and cook for 1 minute, be careful not to burn the garlic.

And the red wine, turn up the heat a fraction to cook out the alcohol, then reduce the liquid by 50 per cent.

Add the carrots, celery, potatoes and sweet potatoes, pour in 275ml of the beef stock and cook for 5 minutes.

Return the beef to the casserole.

Add the remaining stock, Worcestershire sauce, ketchup and bay leaf.

Bring to a boil, cover with the lid, place in the oven and cook for 2 ½ hours. You should check every 30 minutes, adding stock or water if needed.

Once the casserole has been in the oven for 2½ hours, check to see if it needs to cook for a further 30 minutes until the beef is completely tender and the sauce has thickened.

Feel free to remove the lid if you want a thicker stew.

Remove the bay leaf and serve.

LISA'S TIP

For me, this is one of the best dishes of Winter – not only is it nourishing, but it makes the house smell wonderful when it is cooking.

Fish Pie

This healthy take on a traditional recipe is wheat, gluten and dairy-free! The celeriac provides a tasty and low-carb alternative to potatoes and the almond milk replaces milk. Enjoy guilt-free!

{serves 4}

ingredients

2kg celeriac (approx. 2 large), peeled and cut into equal sizes

1 large leek, sliced (keep ¼ layer of leek to wrap the bouquet garni)

1 onion, quartered

1 large bunch of dill

½ celery stalk

7 tbsp coconut oil (virgin or odourless)

3 large eggs

700ml almond milk

500g cod fillets, with skin

500g haddock fillets, with skin

2 tsp horseradish cream, gluten-free

3 tbsp cornflour

¼ tsp nutmeg, ground

sea salt and white pepper

garlic granules

Preparation time - 60 mins, cooking time - 40 mins

Preheat the oven to 375°F, gas mark 5, 190°C (170°C fan-assisted).

Peel celeriac, cut into 5cm cubes and place in a large saucepan. Cover with cold, salted water. Bring to the boil, cover and simmer for 25-30 minutes until tender. Drain and leave to dry in a colander.

In a large non-stick frying pan add 1 tbsp coconut oil and sauté the sliced leeks until soft. Season with sea salt, white pepper and garlic granules then transfer to a bowl with a little finely chopped dill. Boil the eggs, peel and cut into quarters. Set aside.

To make the bouquet garni, place the large bunch of dill in the middle of the celery stalk, wrap in a small layer of leek and tie with string. In the large non-stick frying pan, add the almond milk, bouquet garni and the onion. Put the pan on a low heat until simmering then place the fish fillets into the pan and cook for 5 minutes. Once the fish is cooked, use a slotted spoon to lift the fish onto a plate.

Remove the pan from the heat and let the almond milk infuse for 10 minutes then discard the onion and bouquet garni and strain the milk into a large bowl and set aside. To make the topping of the fish pie, place the celeriac in a food processor and blend until smooth. Add 3 tbsp coconut oil, 2 tsp horseradish, sea salt and white pepper. Check at this point for seasoning.

Creamy sauce - in a large saucepan heat 3 tbsp coconut oil with 3 tbsp cornflour, when it starts to thicken, remove from the heat. Gradually whisk the strained almond milk into the saucepan, it will be thick at first, but keep whisking and a smooth sauce will come together. Return the pan to the heat and whisk until the sauce thickens. Season generously with sea salt, white pepper, and nutmeg. Add the sautéed leeks to the sauce. In a large ovenproof dish 23cm x 23cm, 7cm high, flake the fish (discard the skin) into chunky pieces and place in the base of the dish. Pour over the creamy sauce, and arrange eggs around. Cover with the celeriac purée, smooth out and run the tip of a fork up and down the pie to create a nice topping. Bake the pie in the preheated oven for 40 minutes, or until the top is slightly golden. Leave to stand 10 minutes before serving.

LISA'S TIP

Healthy eating doesn't mean giving up on family favourites. If you are vegetarian or vegan, try substituting cauliflower or broccoli for the fish.

Lamb Curry

A succulent lamb dish made easy
by slow-cooking in the oven.

{serves 4}

ingredients

1kg lamb (from the shoulder), cut into 3cm cubes

250g tomatoes (approx. 2 large), deseeded and cut into thin slices

1 large onion, finely chopped

4 garlic cloves, crushed

400g canned chick peas

400ml chicken stock, gluten-free

2 tbsp rapeseed oil

400ml chicken stock

1 tbsp fresh ginger, grated

1 tbsp cornflour

½ tsp cumin seeds

¼ tsp chilli flakes

1½ tbsp garam masala

1 tsp ground coriander

2 tsp turmeric

sea salt and black pepper

1 tsp tomato purée

1 tsp sugar

garnish

1 handful fresh coriander

160ml coconut cream

wholegrain rice

Preparation time - 30 mins - Cooking time - 2 hour 45 mins

Preheat the oven to 350°F, gas mark 4, 180°C (160°C fan-assisted).

In a food processor blend the chopped onion, garlic, ginger and cumin seeds until smooth.

In a large mixing bowl add the cornflour, chilli flakes, garam masala, turmeric, ground coriander and season with black pepper and sea salt.

Heat a large oval casserole dish (29cm in diameter) and add 1 tbsp rapeseed oil and then the lamb. Cook over a high heat for 3-4 minutes, or until the lamb is golden brown all over, then spoon out the lamb into the seasoned flour mixture, coat the lamb using a spoon until all the pieces are covered with the seasoning.

Reduce the heat and add the remaining oil, add the onion mixture and fry on a gentle heat for about 2-3 minutes, remove the pan from the heat and add the seasoned lamb back to the saucepan.

Cook for a further minute then add the chicken stock slowly to deglaze and release any residue at the bottom of the pan. Bring to a boil, then reduce the heat to a simmer and pour in the coconut milk, sliced deseeded tomatoes, sugar and tomato purée.

Cook covered in the preheated oven for about 1 hour until the lamb is tender.

Reduce the oven temperature to 325°F, gas mark 3, 160°C (140°C fan-assisted) add the chick peas and cook for a further 1 hour and 45 minutes. Check to see if you need to add liquid from time to time.

Just before serving you can add a spoonful or two of coconut cream if you like.

Serve with wholegrain rice and garnish with fresh coriander.

LISA'S TIP
The intense flavours develop overnight so it is best to make ahead!

Mild Chicken Curry

A luscious but light version of chicken
curry flavoured with coconut.

{serves 4 - 6}

ingredients

1 whole chicken, cut into 8 pieces
2 medium onions finely chopped
1 tbsp ground ginger
1 tbsp turmeric
1 tbsp cumin
1 tsp Madras curry powder
2 garlic cloves, minced
2 tbsp peanut oil
50g coconut oil (virgin or
odourless)
12 tbsp soy or coconut yoghurt
400ml coconut milk
2 tsp coconut sugar
sea salt and cracked pepper

garnish

fresh coriander
coconut yogurt (coyo)
wholegrain rice
mango chutney on the side

Preparation time - 40 mins, cooking time - 1.5 to 2 hours (chickens
vary in weight - you may need to adjust cooking time)

Preheat the oven to 350°F, gas mark, 180 °C, (160°C fan-assisted).

Cut legs and thighs from the chicken in one piece, cut legs from
thighs. Cut wings from chicken with a small amount of breast meat,
remove and discard the skin from the chicken. Cut breasts from
chicken, cutting through rib bones along each side of the body, cut
close to the backbone, cut breast into quarters, trim away any excess
fat and retain for sealing the chicken.

Mix the spices together in a bowl, peel and crush the garlic. Place a
frying pan on the stove with a little fat from the chicken and seal the
chicken pieces until lightly coloured on all sides. Place all the seared
chicken pieces on a large roasting tray. Season with sea salt, pepper
and a sprinkle of the spice mix. Add the oil, crushed garlic cloves and
massage into the chicken pieces.

Pour a little coconut oil over each chicken piece and put in the oven,
uncovered, for 30 minutes. In the meantime, chop the onions and
fry over a low heat until soft. Mix the remaining spices together with
the coconut milk, coconut yoghurt, coconut sugar and onions. When
the chicken has been cooking for 30 minutes, take it out of the oven
and pour the coconut milk mixture over the chicken. Cover with the
lid and put back in the oven for another 40-60 minutes, until done,
turning over once, and basting the juices over the chicken. When
cooked, pour in a little coconut yogurt and stir. Garnish with a little
fresh chopped coriander if you wish.

Serve with wholegrain rice and mango chutney.

LISA'S TIP

*Curry can be made 3 days ahead, kept covered in the refrigerator or
can be frozen for up to 2 months. You can replace chicken with other
meat, or turn it into a vegetarian dish. If you have leftovers you can
either chop up the chicken into a coronation chicken salad - just toss in
some lettuce, raisins, flaked almonds and lettuce with a coconut and
mango dressing with a touch of vinegar and off you go!*

Ossobuco

This is my ultimate signature dish! When my family ask 'what's for dinner?' and the answer is Ossobuco, I know there's going to be a full house! Serve with creamy polenta.

{serves 6}

ingredients

8 pieces of veal shin

1 red onion, sliced into half moons

1 white onion, sliced into half moons

4 garlic cloves, minced

75g cornflour

1 tsp vegetable bouillon, gluten-free

1 chicken stock cube, gluten-free

570ml of boiling water

2 tsp honey or agave nectar

4 carrots, sliced lengthways and then sliced in 2

8 tbsp tomato pasta sauce

4 tbsp sweet red wine

4 tbsp olive oil

sea salt, white pepper and cracked black pepper

garlic granules

paprika

garnish

serve with polenta, cook as directed on packaging

Preparation time - 20 mins - Cooking time - 2.5 hours

Preheat the oven to 375°C, gas mark 5, 190°C (170°C fan-assisted).

Wash and pat dry the pieces of veal shin.

Season each piece with garlic granules, paprika, salt and white pepper on both sides on a chopping board.

Lightly cover each piece in cornflour.

In a 29cm casserole dish add the olive oil and fry the onions until soft and translucent, then remove from the dish, fry onions with 2 tbsp olive oil until translucent, then remove from the dish.

Over a gentle heat, seal the veal shins in 2 tbsp olive oil for 20 seconds on each side, then remove onto a plate.

Add the red wine to deglaze the cornflour from the bottom of the dish.

Add the sautéed onions, carrots and crushed garlic, tomato sauce, honey and season with salt and back pepper.

Dissolve the bouillon and chicken stock cube in the boiling water. Add the veal shins to the casserole dish, together with the stock.

Place covered in the oven and bake for 2.5 hours, checking every 50 minutes, turning over the veal and basting the juices.

Serve on a bed of polenta.

LISA'S TIP

At the end of the cooking time, take the lid off to check the meat for tenderness, by gently prodding it with a spoon and remove from the heat but keep warm. This dish is my all time favourite!!! LOVE, LOVE, LOVE (you had me at 'hello' with this dish)!

Raw Tiramisu

The Italian standard elevated
to a decadent level.

{makes 16 slices}

base

200g blanched whole almonds

100g whole almonds (with skins)

150g macadamia nuts

300g soft medjool dates, remove stones

1 tbsp coconut oil (virgin or odourless)

sea salt, pinch

topping

300g cashews, unsalted soaked in water overnight

2 tbsp coconut oil (virgin or odourless)

2 tbsp agave nectar

120ml almond milk

1 tsp vanilla bean paste

2-3 tsp Nescafé espresso freeze dried coffee powder

3-4 tbsp Amaretto liquor

garnish

30g cocoa powder, sifted over the cake

Preparation time - 40 mins, soaking (8 hours) plus freezing time 2 -3 hours

Soak the cashews overnight for 8 hours with enough water to cover (this method helps to soften and blend well to get the creamy texture).

Line the base and sides of a square 8 ½ inch by 8 ½ inch loose bottom tin with parchment paper.

In a food processor blend the almonds and macadamia nuts until roughly chopped, then pour into a mixing bowl.

Remove the stones from the medjool dates and place into the food processor, blend until smooth.

When the dates are smooth add the coconut oil and a pinch of sea salt together with roughly chopped almonds and macadamia nuts and blend until combined (do not over blend, as you want to keep a little texture to the base).

Press this mixture into the base of your tin, then smooth out with the back of a spoon until completely level.

Then place in the freezer to harden up whilst you make the filling.

Pass the cashews, which have been soaked overnight, through a sieve and run under cold water, then drain on kitchen towel to remove excess water.

To make the filling in the food processor, add the soaked cashew nuts and blend for 3 minutes until smooth, wipe down the sides with a spatula, add the coconut oil and blend for a further 2 minutes, keep wiping down the sides so all the cashews are blended.

In a measuring jug, add the almond milk, agave nectar, coconut oil, coffee (I used 2 tsp. coffee, although you can add more), amaretto (I used 3 tbsp. amaretto, although you can add more) and vanilla bean paste.

Beat the mixture with a small hand whisk or fork so that everything is thoroughly blended.

LISA'S TIP

I love tiramisu. Seriously...it's the perfect not too sweet, light and creamy treat - dessert does not have to be a guilt ridden pleasure. This one is delicious and full of precious nutrients and it's wonderful as it's dairy free, with no added preservatives or additives. Do not eat the whole thing in one sitting though. I know, it is going to be very tempting!

Blend the cashew mixture again, slowly pouring in the milk mixture until everything is combined, check for taste - you might need to add more coffee or amaretto.

Remove the base from the freezer, then carefully spoon the mixture into the tin, make sure again that the filling is smooth and level.

Place back in the freezer for 2-3 hours.

When ready to serve, remove from the freezer, sprinkle with sifted cocoa powder and garnish with chocolate shavings.

Cut into 16 slices when you're ready to serve. You can either keep this dessert in the freezer or the refrigerator.

Gluten-free Chocolate Banana Cake

A real showstopper with its crushed banana chips and
shaved chocolate. The frosting is dairy-free too.

{serves 12}

ingredients

1 tsp espresso coffee powder

1 tsp boiling water

4 large eggs, beaten

175g coconut sugar

1 tsp vanilla bean paste

100g fine cornmeal

150g dark chocolate, melted

2 ripe bananas, mashed

chocolate covering

200g dark chocolate melted

50g coconut oil (virgin or
odourless)

250ml soya single cream

80g banana chips, crushed

Preparation time - 30 mins, cooking time - 30 mins, decorating time 30 mins

Preheat the oven to 310°F, gas mark 3, 160°C (140°C fan-assisted).

Rub some oil on 2 x 20cm (8inch) round cake tins and line the base with parchment paper.

Dissolve the espresso coffee powder with the boiling water, set aside. Melt the chocolate in a glass bowl over hot simmering water. Then set aside to cool. Beat the eggs and coconut sugar with an electric beater until light and fluffy. Add the vanilla bean paste and coffee mixture. Gradually add the fine cornmeal to the egg mixture.

When the chocolate has cooled, add the mashed bananas. Fold the chocolate and mashed bananas into the egg mixture until combined. Divide the mixture between the two cake tins and bake on the middle shelf for 30 minutes. Remove from the oven and leave to cool in the tins for 10 minutes, then turn out onto a wire rack to cool, then either cover tightly with foil or continue to decorate.

To make the icing, melt the chocolate as above, then slightly cool and stir in the coconut oil and then the cream. To assemble the chocolate covering, place one half of the cake on your serving platter. Using a palette knife, spread a layer of the chocolate icing on the cake, then sandwich together.

Cover the sides and top of the cake with the icing carefully with a warmed palette knife. Fill in any gaps. The sides/top should be straight and even. Scatter the crushed banana chips around the sides of the cake and decorate the top with chocolate shavings. Allow the cake to sit at room temperature, covered by a cake dome or a large glass bowl, for at least two hours before serving. The flavours will improve and get better with time.

LISA'S TIP

This is a lovely, moist cake, which is sometimes hard to achieve with gluten-free flour! When you pull the cake out of the oven, it will look like it's not done in the centre. Don't worry, that's correct!

Florentines

The combination of dried fruits, cornflakes, all held together by sweetened condensed milk is magic to the taste buds. For extra indulgence why not coat the base or drizzle the top with melted white, milk or dark chocolate.

....

{makes 40 - 50}

ingredients

250g corn flakes, gluten-free
200g salted peanuts
200g raisins
397g condensed milk

chocolate covering

50g dark chocolate, melted

Preparation time - 40 mins, cooking time - 12 to 13 mins

Preheat the oven to 325°F, gas mark 3, 170°C (150°C fan-assisted).

Line two large baking trays with parchment paper.

In a large mixing bowl add the cornflakes, raisins & salted peanuts.

Pour over the condensed milk. Using a wooden spoon carefully ensure that the corn flakes are coated with the condensed milk.

I use 30g of mixture and a teacup to make the Florentines. Using a teaspoon, press mixture into the base. Then flip onto your pre-lined baking tray (occasionally dip the cup into a bowl of cold water to help the Florentines slide out).

Bake in the preheated oven for 12-13 minutes, watching to ensure that they don't burn.

Remove from the oven, leave to cool on the tray then transfer to a wire rack to cool completely.

Melt the dark chocolate in a bain marie (a saucepan of boiling water over a hob on medium/high heat, the chocolate goes in a bowl over the saucepan, not touching the hot water).

Drizzle the melted chocolate over the Florentines.

LISA'S TIP

These are a favourite festive delight, that will quickly be devoured at any time in our household. A great treat for children to get involved in making and they don't cost a lot too! If you find making the Florentines too technical, you can line the sides and base of 25cm square tin with parchment paper and press the mixture into the tin and bake, then you can cut into squares.

Raw Chocolate Mousse Cake

A silky mousse cake with a crunchy base and the
wonderful flavours of chocolate and coconut.

{serves 12 -14}

crust ingredients

100g pistachio nuts

150g blanched almonds

50g desiccated coconut

200g dates (pre soak if hard)

3 tsp lemon juice

1 pinch sea salt

chocolate covering

200g dark chocolate

2 x 400ml coconut milk, full fat
canned (keep refrigerated)

1 x 160ml coconut cream (keep
refrigerated), reserve 2 tsp for
garnish

3 tbsp date syrup

2 tsp custard powder

garnish

2 tsp coconut cream, whipped
taken from above

Preparation time - 60 mins, freezing time 20 mins.

Line the base and sides of 20cm non-stick springform tin with
parchment paper.

Place the pistachios, blanched almonds and desiccated coconut into
a food processor and pulse until a chunky sandy consistency. Place
into a clean bowl. Add the dates, lemon juice and salt to the food
processor, blend until smooth.

Add the pistachio nut mixture back into the food processor, and
blend until it forms a ball. Place the nut and date mixture into your
prepared tin, press down firmly on the base and one inch around the
sides and place in the freezer. Remove the coconut milk cans from the
fridge, turn them upside down and open the 'wrong end' up (the milk
will separate from the cream in the fridge). Pass the coconut milk
and cream through a sieve (you only want to use the hard part of the
coconut, discard the milk for this recipe). Spoon into a food mixer or
use an electric hand held whisk. Beat for about 4-5 minutes, stopping
occasionally to wipe down the side of the bowl.

Melt the chocolate, over a water bath for one minute then add the
date syrup and custard powder. Leave to cool then add the cream.
Slowly fold the cream mixture into the chocolate, mix well (keeping 2
tsp of the whipped cream aside). If the chocolate gets hard and gritty
when folding in the whipped coconut cream, don't panic, just place
the bowl back over the water bath and stir until smooth.

Remove the nut base after 20 minutes from the freezer. When the
chocolate mixture is smooth, pour into the nut base. Smooth out the
chocolate mixture. Drizzle 2 tsp whipped coconut cream over the top
of the chocolate mousse and then, using a toothpick, carefully mix up
the coconut cream into the chocolate to get a marble effect.

Keep refrigerated once made.

LISA'S TIP

*If you LOVE chocolate as much as I do, then this is for you. Yes it
is possible to prepare the chocolate mousse from only a couple of
ingredients without dairy, cream or eggs! Make sure you refrigerate the
cans of coconut milk and cream overnight to solidify and separate.*

Recipe Index

Autumn

Winter

Acknowledgements

To my wonderful family,

Thanks to all of you who have contributed their time, knowledge and experience and taken on duties of chief tasters…

My gratitude and thanks go to the following people in no particular order for their support, encouragement and inspiration.

Mum, Dad my dedication says it all, although here is another place to say thank you for believing in this exciting adventure. Grandma Jackie, you've been such an instrumental figure in my life, like a second mum to me, thank you for sharing your recipes and enjoying my cakes, even if they have been gluten-free (although I think I have finally converted you!). To my brother Danny Roukin, thank you for all your constructive criticism, and I have noted when you're around 'not too much salt or sugar'! To my sister-in-law Liat Roukin, thank you for always being happy to receive food deliveries in return for your feedback, and I look forward to cooking with my nephews, Eitan & Ori Roukin. To my close cousins who have played a very important role in my life. Thank you Michelle Burns being a 'sister', you've been through my ups and downs, yet you've always been there for me and we've shared fabulous food around the world together. Thank you to another 'sister', Rebekah 'Shaman' Bloom for her continued support, encouragement and inspiration. Thank you to Jo and Mitch Kaye for being my first students and their continued enthusiasm. Thank you, Harriet and David Bloom, for always believing in me. Thank you Lawrence Bloom, Janet Bloom, Lynda Burns and all my extended family for your ongoing loving support.

To my wonderful family and friends, so many of you have helped me throughout the good and bad times, although I think it has made our relationships stronger. Thank you for also being my chief tasters, Abi and Gemma Rogers, I can always count on one of the Rogers sisters liking one of my recipes! Thank you Samantha Norman for our long walks and talks about food and relationships. Thank you Emma Eker for your valuable knowledge and support. Thank you Katie Waxman for your love and being a strategy sounding board. Thank you to my dinner party girls, Charlotte Bentley, Vicky Baruch and Samantha Richards, for sharing delicious food and great chats.

Huge thank you to my special friend Kemal Alam, you've been influential from the beginning.

A further thank you to Tammy Poggo, Jo Brook, Sasha Cedar, Denise Peters, Sasha Goldsmith, Tracey Wander, Matt Florin, Marcelo Sanchez, Sacha Isaacs, Marc Lewis, Lex Van Dam, Leonard Charlton, Tanya Selkus, Lisette Lewis, Hilary Natoff, Xenia Capsalis, Sam Hill, Perry Field and Lisa Halpern.

To my wonderful team who've brought this cookbook to life. Thank you. Tracey Tannenbaum for stepping into my shoes; you've been my personal guardian and you've delivered my story in such a beautiful way. To my team at Spiffing Covers, James Willis, Richard Chalkley and Stefan Proudfoot, thank you all for your creativity and pulling this whole book together, I may have driven you mad at times, but we made it happen. To my food photographer, David Munns, as soon as I saw your incredible talented work, I knew you were the best person for this cookbook; everyone is already salivating over

Acknowledgements

your amazing pictures. Thank you Victoria Allen for the use of your amazing props, I was immensely upset to return everything! A massive thank you to my food stylist, Emily Kydd, my lifesaver, so talented and made all my recipes with love and brought them to life. Thank you Rina Steinberg, my make-up artist for making me look refreshed and glowing, if only you could make me up every day! Thank you to my wardrobe stylist Jude Lobb, for styling me in a comfortable and stylish, elegant way (loving my new wardrobe)! You have all been extremely talented and supportive in your own areas and I most certainly couldn't have wished for a better team. I couldn't have done this book without you all.

To my pillars of support for wisdom, guidance and encouragement when I needed reassurance, a huge thanks to KP for influencing me that life is not a sprint it's a marathon. Thank you, Dr. Eric Ansell and Linda Swimer, you've both independently encouraged me to believe in myself.

To my past employers who taught me all the learning curves of business, my deepest appreciation goes to where my career and love of food started with Sylvia & Harold Sobell, Sara Quah, Elayne Mattey, Tony Page, Melvyn Bentley, Jesus Adorno, Natalia Andreyeva and Daniel Herman.

To all the professional chefs & suppliers who have graciously and generously donated their time or their produce. Thank you to Ocado for providing all the ingredients for the *My Relationship with Food* cookbook - Neill Abrams, Arati Nar and Drew Norton. Thank you to my suppliers for their reliable service and advice, Yossi at Menachem, Bifulco Butchers, Dominic at JA Corney and John at Panzers Fruit. Thank you to my chef friends Michael Wilding, Dona & Duarte Silva for sharing enthusiasm for recipes and tips.

To my students and institutes who have supported me, thank you to Barbara Mansi, Helen Harris and Anne Melbourne for giving me the opportunity to teach at HGSI, encouraging students to cook. Teaching cookery is like a story. You have wonderful ingredients, a method and then finishing creating something made with love.

Thank you to my students who've enjoyed being taught and for your emails and testimonials. Glad to hear you are continuing to cook my recipes! You can now have 100 recipes in one place! Danielle Sehayek, Simone Suss, Debbie Fireman, Deborah Roberts, Sharon Pollins, Barry Cohen, Elaine French, Jules Gishen, Michael Angel, Janine Asserson, Hazel Avigdori, Libby Avigdori, Mike Leibling, Dafna Reynolds, Renata Grgek, Laura Hilton, Louise Robey and Daniel Levin and a special thank you to Laurence Field and Rachel Creeger at the LJCC to giving me all the wonderful opportunities of working closely with Fusion children's cookery programs and setting up 'The FUSION Gateways Programme' and huge thank you to Victoria Prever, for your guidance and for featuring my recipes in the JC Newspaper.

To anyone I have left out, I am sorry although I am happy to sign your cookbook with a personalized acknowledgement with my gratitude.

Lisa x

I'd love to see how your cooking turns out so make sure to tag #myrelationshipwithfood when posting your pics!

 @myrelationshipwithfood

 @cookwithlisa

 myrelationshipwithfood

 lisa@myrelationshipwithfood